Eugenics in American Political Life

Shannon Bow O'Brien

Eugenics in American Political Life

How the Politics of Superiority Still Shape Us Today

Shannon Bow O'Brien
The University of Texas at Austin
Austin, TX, USA

ISBN 978-3-031-63552-6   ISBN 978-3-031-63553-3 (eBook)
https://doi.org/10.1007/978-3-031-63553-3

© The Editor(s) (if applicable) and The Author(s), under exclusive license to Springer Nature Switzerland AG 2024

This work is subject to copyright. All rights are solely and exclusively licensed by the Publisher, whether the whole or part of the material is concerned, specifically the rights of translation, reprinting, reuse of illustrations, recitation, broadcasting, reproduction on microfilms or in any other physical way, and transmission or information storage and retrieval, electronic adaptation, computer software, or by similar or dissimilar methodology now known or hereafter developed.
The use of general descriptive names, registered names, trademarks, service marks, etc. in this publication does not imply, even in the absence of a specific statement, that such names are exempt from the relevant protective laws and regulations and therefore free for general use.
The publisher, the authors and the editors are safe to assume that the advice and information in this book are believed to be true and accurate at the date of publication. Neither the publisher nor the authors or the editors give a warranty, expressed or implied, with respect to the material contained herein or for any errors or omissions that may have been made. The publisher remains neutral with regard to jurisdictional claims in published maps and institutional affiliations.

Cover illustration: © Melisa Hasan

This Palgrave Macmillan imprint is published by the registered company Springer Nature Switzerland AG
The registered company address is: Gewerbestrasse 11, 6330 Cham, Switzerland

If disposing of this product, please recycle the paper.

I would like to dedicate this book to my husband, Bill O'Brien. Your endless support means the world.

Preface

The very first upper-division undergraduate class I taught was urban politics. The book I assigned had a section on the Progressive Era. Though the book focused on political reforms, I also wanted to integrate social events of the era. I developed a section on eugenics that discussed its impact on the Progressive Era within American politics. This material was primarily historical for the first ten years I taught the class. Many students had never heard of eugenics, and it was a short introduction to the concept.

Around 2015, the topic began to feel less historical and more current. It is odd to teach a class where you know the material is dated, yet it feels less so every semester. Generally, we update material because it ages and needs revision. It hits entirely differently when you revise to ensure you avoid too many modern comparisons at that point during the semester.

Eugenics became a topic that grew more current with every semester. During the Trump administration, I began to regularly field questions in class about early twentieth-century immigration law's application to now. Lectures about America's past began to get far closer attention from the students than I had ever seen. Ideas started lingering around, leading me to ask other questions. Before I knew it, I was reading old books and realizing much of our past was still very salient to our politics, especially our politicians.

This book is the product of classes and questions. The more I learn about politics, political science, history, science, and everything else, the less I feel I know. Every year, I feel smaller standing in front of the vast libraries of knowledge in this world. There will never be enough time, enough days, or enough moments to learn everything. If I am exceedingly lucky, I will be able to become a little bit more knowledgeable about a few things during my scant time on this planet. This endeavor reflects my attempt to bring order to the ideas within my mind about eugenics.

Eugenics is, was, and always has been about power. People in power make the rules for a society. More important, those same people in power want to retain their hegemony. There are many paths to staying in power. Some people engage in conflict, but others prefer less direct approaches. In my doctoral program, a lecture from Dr. Kenneth D. Wald always stuck with me. He explained that voting was similar to light switches. If you have two people from opposing parties who both turn on their lights, they engage in a zero-sum game by canceling each other out. A more successful candidate convinces their base to turn on their light while simultaneously convincing the other party it is not worth their time or energy. You can ensure your win while avoiding conflict. Granted, at the time, Dr. Wald was discussing elections, but it has become one of those significant ideas I linger over when I think about motivations. Eugenics, in many ways, functions in an almost identical way. People in power believe they are the only ones worthy of retaining it. The easiest and least conflictual way to hold onto this power involves co-opting others into thinking they are unworthy stewards. Laws, statuary, and rhetoric all frame a society in ways that mold it to reinforce these ideas.

The development of this book, in many ways, starts with Richard Neustadt. He famously said, "presidential power is the power to persuade" (Neustadt, 1960, p. vi). For the president, the most potent tool involves his ability to convince others to support his ideas. My last book, *Donald Trump and the Kayfabe Presidency*, started when I realized Trump used wrestling rhetoric and tactics to sway the public. He used tools recognized by his base but foreign to traditional politicians within America. Throughout the Trump administration, I would hear and see policies and language that felt like material I would reference in my classes on eugenics. The more I saw, the more I read up on earlier period scholarship. I think that Donald Trump uses the persuasion power of the presidency to push for policies and attitudes that are more in line with those of late nineteenth and early twentieth-century eugenicists.

His policy proposals, plans, and platforms are well-thought-out and intentional appeals that blend entertainment and eugenical thought.

Tactics honed from decades of wrestling showmanship influence crowds into abeyance. They understand and react to the tropes of persecuted protagonists beset by naysayers and detractors. They revel in the hyperbole, patting themselves on their backs since they consider themselves 'smart marks.' In wrestling vernacular, smart marks are the fans who understand it is scripted and revel in their insider knowledge. Donald Trump exploits their beliefs, though in reality, he treats them as simply marks, counting on them to blindly follow his lead without question.

This book attempts to blend historical and current political ideas to help understand how the old is new again. Additionally, the past is never truly forgotten but often given a new veneer. Many of Donald Trump's platforms and promises are older ideas grounded in early twentieth-century eugenics. They have been rewrapped and presented again like a regifted fondue set someone pulled out of the attic from the distant past. It is old enough that people cannot remember it, so they believe it is new when it is the castoffs from a previous generation.

The purpose and scope of this book involve trying to explain how eugenics developed and how its ideas impacted and still impact America. These chapters highlight prominent authors, advocates, and persons who help push forward ideas of the superiority of White Nordic nativism within American life. The first chapter tries to provide an overview of eugenics. It explains many of the foundations of the ideas, significant influences, and influencers. Many of these ideas are impacted by the sweeping influence Calvinism held over early America. The idea that a person's character and eventual eternal destination are decided even before their birth helps lend credence to the chosen within a society. The chapter discusses how early twentieth-century ideals and social life shaped American culture and encouraged attitudes toward racial and ethnic biases. The chapter then introduces how certain eugenicists held sway over immigration policies in that period. It also explores how state fairs helped promote and mainstream eugenic ideas throughout the United States.

The second chapter explores faithful slave statuary in America during the early twentieth century. In particular, it explores the popularization of memorializing Southern Mammies leading up to the eventual failure of a bill in the U.S. Congress to authorize a Mammy statue in Washington, D.C. At first glance, this chapter may feel disjointed, but the ideas are intertwined with eugenics within American life. Moreover, the push for this statue occurs while Congress is holding hearings over immigration restrictions with eugenics displays in their halls. This chapter aims to help weave together how political rights and these statues exist within the same space. The persons advocating for Mammy statues simultaneously push forward ideas restricting minority political participation. The movement's growth behind these statues is essential and often not considered. Subservient statuary was a way to provide generational object lessons of the only acceptable roles for Black persons within American society. At the same time, immigration hearings were lamenting the inferiority of foreign populations, calling for severe restrictions.

The third chapter picks up the theme of immigration restrictions within the first two chapters and explores it more carefully. This chapter looks at the early origins of colonists in America and how many arrived as indentured servants, especially as transported felons. The United Kingdom sent its unwanted criminal population here for generations as a way to remove them from their shores. Our founding has been carefully rebranded as one filled with freedom-seeking pilgrims, not forcibly relocated reprobates. As we forged our new nation, America swept away the more uncomfortable aspects of many former British subjects. It fashioned a new narrative of virtuous, superior people inundated by problematic immigrants. Restrictive immigration policies emerged, cumulating with the Immigration Act of 1924. Eugenicists lobbied and argued for this act, framing it as a battle for the very soul of America.

The fourth chapter looks at Donald Trump's rhetoric from a eugenic lens. This chapter examines specific statements and quotes Donald Trump made as a presidential candidate and sitting president. These are contextualized with language, phrases, and classic, influential writings by early twentieth-century eugenicists. Many of Donald Trump's statements parrot these authors and closely follow their logic. This chapter looks at Trump's words regarding immigration, abortion policy, health, fitness, and religion, as well as other areas, comparing and pointing out similarities to early advocates of eugenics and others who bemoaned race suicide. The chapter also explores many slurs and derisive monikers Donald Trump attaches to other people. There is a clear delineation of how he addresses people negatively. Women of color receive intentional, personalized, targeted language, often assigning alliterative terms that dog whistle as well as demean. The chapter shows how Donald Trump's language and rhetoric are not innovative but heavily draw upon others' ideas to evoke strong connections to America's eugenic past.

Many of the authors used in this book were icons in their days. They faded from prominence and turned into footnotes of history. Their biases and bigotry toward any person outside their narrow definitions was dismissed as inadequate, inferior, and undeserving of equality. Donald Trump's beliefs and policies echo their thoughts so closely that their points of view have been resuscitated and resurrected to be placed again in the center of American thought. However, their names, Madison Grant, Harry H. Laughlin, Lothrop Stoddard, Ira Calvin, Francis Galton, and many others, have been stripped away, leaving only their ideas in place. When journalists or commentators compare Donald Trump to Adolph Hitler, it is inaccurate and unfair. Hitler and the Third Reich borrowed their ideals of racial purity from the United States. It is far more accurate to look at what they were reading in its original English and see how that influenced the positions of Donald Trump.

Austin, USA   Shannon Bow O'Brien

Reference

Neustadt, R.E. (1960). *Presidential Power, the Politics of Leadership*. Wiley.

Acknowledgments

I have taught a class on Urban Politics since 2003. It has always had a section on eugenics. I want to thank all my students over the years for putting up with my lectures, especially those who would ask questions, push me on material, and make me a better scholar. Many people deserve thanks. First, one of my best friends, Jacob R. Straus, for his patience, willingness to listen to me play with ideas, and ability to always know the best way to look up something when I'm stuck on a research question. I have always truly valued his friendship, and I'm better because of knowing him. Michael Anderson, on my hall at Texas, has always had a friendly ear and insightful commentary as I worked through ideas. He has been an excellent person to throw ideas around with to see if they are worth pursuing. Nyah Patel is a fantastic person who is often wise beyond her years. Nyah was my research assistant in the spring semester of 2023. I had several questions about material that ultimately became part of Chapter 2. Nyah took on the challenge of researching the statues and helping find some supporting evidence for the ideas I was chasing down. I look forward to seeing how amazing her life turns out. I'd also like to thank Yu Ouyang at Purdue Northwest for letting me present the early ideas of this book in a paper at the American Political Science Association's annual meeting. Selling eugenics to presidential scholars can be challenging, and he has always supported my research.

From 2021–2023, my husband was an AAAS fellow in Washington, D.C., for the Department of Energy. His experience allowed me access to the District of Columbia resources during academic breaks. I could research old newsletters and pamphlets at the Library of Congress. Conducting research in their main reading room in that fantastic atmosphere was a joy of a lifetime. The proposal for this project was written primarily at two libraries. The Martin Luther King Jr location of the D.C. Public Library has terrific views and great places to tuck away and work. The Aurora Hills location of the Arlington Public Library was close to our apartment and offered quiet workplaces. I sincerely appreciated both locations since two adults in a small apartment with one working remote is challenging. The one on summer break often needed to vacate for a quiet place to work, and public libraries are excellent locations.

On that note, I would also like to acknowledge and thank the University of Texas's Perry-Castañeda (PCL) library. The bulk of this project involves materials that are almost a century old. The resources at our PCL library are unparalleled. It is the best university library I have ever worked in as a student or scholar. The depth of their collection made me fist pump when I was trying to locate an obscure piece of work and find it in our physical or digital collections. This book simply would not have been possible without the PCL library. As I write this section, I look at the literal mini-library of their books surrounding my desk. This library is a treasure and asset to the university, and I am very grateful for it.

I'd also like to acknowledge my brother Jonathan. I value his ideas and insights, and I'm proud of the person he has become. I'm honored to know him.

I'm sure I'm missing many people I have talked to over the years about these ideas. I sincerely thank you for putting up with my ideas and enthusiasm for obscure authors and how they still impact us today.

About This Book

The book focuses on the power of eugenics. It explores how the language and ideas of famous eugenicists still impact us today. Their ideas, thoughts, and beliefs shaped and continue to shape our world. They influence our ideas about immigration, acceptance, and belonging within America. The book explores eugenics and its importance in American development. It looks at the early origins of eugenics and how it mainstreamed into America. It looks at how these ideas impacted the proliferation of faithful slaves or Mammy statues. Many of the advocates for these statues were political figures who were simultaneously working to curtail minority political participation. The push for a statue in Washington, DC, intersected with hearings about immigration policy from prominent eugenicists. The book looks at many English arrived as transported felons and transitioned into an American identity. Restrictive immigration policies grew out of eugenic concerns about the racial and ethnic composition of the United States. Donald Trump's rhetoric suggests he embraces many positions stridently advocated by early 20th-century American eugenicists. The book examines what he says and how closely it follows policy platforms adopted by American eugenicists, such as making clear distinctions between citizens and subjects within a society.

Contents

1	**Eugenics Origins**	1
	Early Developments	3
	Calvinism	7
	Muscular Christianity and Race Suicide	9
	Eugenics in Mainstream	11
	Fitter Family & Better Baby Contests	12
	Sideshows as Object Lessons	15
	Framing the Outdoors as Healthy to Contrast with Urban Immigration	16
	Eugenics Turns to Immigration Policy	17
	The Impact Harry H. Laughlin	19
	Why Does It Still Matter?	20
	References	22
2	**Mammy Statues, Power, and the Importance of Framing**	27
	Robert Love Taylor	28
	James Thomas "Cotton Tom" Heflin	31
	The Usage of Mammy to Craft Acceptable Social Roles	33
	Why Does Statuary Matter?	35
	How Titles Signal Power	36
	Mammy Memorial at the National Level	37
	Confederate Memorial at Arlington National Cemetery	37

National Mammy Statue	40
Other Memorials and Memory	43
The Intersection of Mammy Statues and Immigration Legislation	46
Conclusion	47
References	49
3 Immigration Laws and Eugenics	55
Foundational Immigration	56
Immigration Moving Forward	61
The Emergence of Americans	63
Restrictive Immigration Policies	64
Conclusion	71
References	71
4 Donald Trump's Rhetoric and How Eugenics Frames His World	75
Genetic Superiority	77
Immigrants and Controlling Birth	84
Immigrants and Non-American Populations	87
Trump and His Use of Mocking and Slurs	94
What Is the Purpose of a Slur?	95
Donald Trump, Fit, Health, and Religion	98
Conclusion	101
References	102
5 Conclusion	113
References	119
Index	121

About the Author

Shannon Bow O'Brien, Ph.D. is an Associate Professor of Instruction at the University of Texas at Austin in the Government Department. She specializes in American Politics with an emphasis on American presidency and political development. She has a bachelor's and a master's from the University of Louisville and her PhD from the University of Florida.

Her research has two primary areas of focus: presidential speeches and early American development. She is very interested in presidential speechmaking. Her book, *Why Presidential Speech Locations Matter: Analyzing Speechmaking from Truman to Obama* was published in 2018. She believes you can develop a better understanding of administration priorities and actions by looking the later patterns of places they choose to spend time. Her 2020 book, *Donald Trump and the Kayfabe Presidency: Professional Wrestling Rhetoric in the White House*, explores the president's usage of theatrical language for rhetorical and political advantage.

She and her husband live in Austin, Texas.

CHAPTER 1

Eugenics Origins

Abstract This chapter provides an overview of the development of eugenics as an idea and how it grew within society. Many of these ideas are impacted by the sweeping influence Calvinism held over early America and how that helped set up a country receptive to eugenic ideas. The chapter discusses how early twentieth-century ideals and social life shaped American culture and encouraged attitudes toward racial and ethnic biases. The chapter then introduces how certain eugenicists held sway over immigration policies in that period. It also discusses how these ideas were mainstreamed into America with exhibitions at fairs, often in agricultural areas.

Keywords Eugenics · Race suicide · Calvinism · Fitter families · Immigration

The word eugenics conjures up a variety of images. Frequently, people associate the term with Nazis and their policies of extermination during the Second World War. However, eugenics describes a much broader movement of late nineteenth to early twentieth-century social policy within the United Kingdom and the United States. Many of the German Reich's laws were adapted from existing American laws. Americans educated in schools before the Second World War were exposed to

© The Author(s), under exclusive license to Springer Nature Switzerland AG 2024
S. B. O'Brien, *Eugenics in American Political Life*,
https://doi.org/10.1007/978-3-031-63553-3_1

1

these ideas as mainstream policy. Aspects permeated American life in a considerable number of ways. American culture embraced and accepted eugenic principles as scientifically and socially sound. These were taught in schools and universities as dominant theories to explain desirable hereditary outcomes. These have shaped our worldviews and outlooks for decades. The language and intentions of eugenics still surround us today. The policies of political actors echo these approaches in their contemporary rhetoric. While they strip the word eugenics from their politics, it is still there as the unstated reality. The quiet part of their policies is not said out loud. It exists in the stereotypes, euphemisms, and colorless dismissals.

Within modern society, eugenics has become synonymous with Germany's Third Reich. Nazism has become the boogeyman that haunts the corners of history. Nazis have been used so frequently as hyperbole that they have become an avatar for evil. We use Hitler or Nazi when we want to draw a comparison to something so awful it should not be given any purchase. Overuse and exaggerated comparisons have watered down the claims to nothingness. The accusation of speaking like Hitler or acting like the Nazis typically results in an eye-roll followed by an allegation of outrageous dramatics without actual evidence. In addition, these complaints also deflect attention away from the fact the Third Reich borrowed many ideas from American laws and groups that advocated eugenics. American culture holds up Nazism as an ultimate expression of wrongness while exhibiting societal amnesia from where they got many of the ideas in the first place. Americans clutch their pearls in anger over policies innovated initially by their people and governments. They cringe at the terms like eugenics and Nazis as slurs, while many still advocate for the same fundamental goals and intentions of their original work. Americans carefully strip out the words, feigning anger at comparison while retaining the same goals of a curated society within their preferred images.

This chapter examines some foundations and how eugenics is engrained into American life. These concepts became integral to our thinking, helping fuel antagonism toward others we perceive as threats. Eugenics became such a part of American culture in many places that we no longer remember its roots or see the prevalence of its legacy in our daily lives. More importantly, when we have modern politicians like Donald Trump advocating for sweeping racial and ethnic immigration restrictions, many do not realize those beliefs are rooted in this earlier era.

When these restrictions are coupled with broad depictions evoking fear-mongering cloaked as invasions or other dangers, people do not recognize the older eugenic origins of those phrases.

Eugenics is complicated, nuanced, and messy. Scientists wanted to develop better ways to improve society. However, eugenics approached societal problems from deliberately biased approaches. It used genetics toward predetermined goals while purposely ignoring social components. Scholars attributed all aspects of a person's being to their blood and genetic history while ignoring upbringing or situations. Solitary exemplars would be elevated if they were the vanguard of confirmation bias while disregarding mountains of other examples that may act as counterfactuals.

Early Developments

Francis Galton creates the term eugenics, combining the Greek word good (eu) with the root of creation/beginning (genesis) and adding a suffix (Stern, 2005, p. 11). Galton first uses the term in his 1883 book, *Inquiries into Human Faculty and Its Development*. Francis Galton and Charles Darwin were first cousins, the former inspired by the latter. Darwin's *On the Origin of the Species* in 1859 inspired Galton to write his own work. Galton wanted to expand on his relative's ideas while making a name for himself within the field. His portmanteau of Greek words was intentional. He was influenced by Plato's *Republic V*, which in an 1852 translation, says "the best of both sexes ought to be brought together as often as possible, and the worst seldom as possible, and that the issue of the former unions ought to be reared, and that of the latter abandoned, if the flock is to attain first-rate excellence; and these proceedings ought to be kept a secret from all but the magistrates themselves..." (Davies & Vaughan, 1935, 167). Mary Brown (1935) in *An Introduction to Eugenics* asserts Plato "suggested that the state intervene to mate the best with the best, and the worst with the worst and these children of the unfit were to be "put away in some mysterious, unknown places as they should be" (p. 16). This passage by Plato helps substantiate the idea that better selection creates better results. The science of the 'good born' became an obsession for many academics, politicians, and influential citizens. It shapes our world through laws, thoughts, and basic ways we consider persons worthy of existing within the world. Galton develops the term eugenics, but Charles Davenport (1911) gives it its most succinct definition by referring to it as "the science of the improvement of the human race by better breeding" (Stern, 2005, p. 11).

Though it does sound unusual to modern readers, early eugenics tackled their contemporary issues from a not unreasonable place. As early as 1865, we can see how Galton's thinking may have been influenced by Darwin and that passage from Plato, which also discussed the breeding of farm animals. In *Hereditary Talent and Character*, Francis Galton writes, "If a twentieth part of the cost and pains were spent in measures for the improvement of the human race that is spent on the improvement of the breed of horses and cattle, what a galaxy of genius we might not create!" (p. 165). Early researchers saw the shortcomings of their society. In particular, the struggles of how poor urban living impacted children. Some observed similarities among children who exhibited mental or physical shortcomings. Addiction and poverty were seen as consequences of inferiority rather than intersectionality of circumstances.

Karl Pearson (1912), in *The Groundwork for Eugenics*, asserts that "alcoholism in the parent was one of the chief sources of mental defect in children" (pp. 5–6). At the Medico-Psychological Association of Great Britain and Ireland, eugenics was called a 'chief remedy' to problems of heredity, and "Legislation aiming at the control of alcoholism and venereal disease was next advocated, and as a further measure the State supervision and care over the defective classes" (Medico-Psychological, 1906, p. 259). The Eugenics Laboratory (later the Galton Laboratory) at University College London began collecting family histories and reporting diseases (Heron, 1907). They noted, "mentally defective offspring occur in families in which neuroses, alcoholism, or insanity are more or less frequent" (Heron, 1907, p. 6). In 1910, Ethel M. Elderton published *A First Study of the Influence of Parental Alcoholism on the Physique and Ability of Offspring* (Elderton, 1910). It was quickly followed up by a similarly named second study (Pearson & Elderton, 1910). These works, along with other researchers working on similar projects (Howard, 1910), tied parental alcohol consumption to deficiencies within their children.

These early roots of eugenics matter because of the questions they were addressing. At their core, these works were trying to investigate the causes and then effects of alcoholism upon individuals and their children. They understood the generalities of inheritance but lacked the understanding of modern science in the interplay of environmental and genetic factors. Many of the impacts they explore are now attributed to what we refer to as Fetal Alcohol Spectrum Disorders (FASDs) or, sometimes, Fetal Alcohol Syndrome ("Fetal Alcohol," n.d.; Mayo Clinic Staff, 2018). FASDs can have physical and behavioral concerns that can follow a person throughout the entirety of their life. These early researchers identified and used tools available to describe and diagnose it. They recognized that alcohol usage resulted in detrimental impacts upon children but conflated medical concerns with environmental trauma. FASD and parental social actions were considered part of the same whole.

Eugenics' goals quickly shifted away from shortcomings caused by alcohol and toward developing broader theories that promote ways to improve people. The research moved into advancing genetic ideals by systematically eliminating undesirable traits. Most of this research was never more complicated than basic Mendel genetics with Punnett squares. Yet, it was embraced to explain all aspects of a person's physical appearance and personality traits. Alcoholism continued to be linked to eugenics even into the 1940s. Pamphlets published by the Eugenics Society of Northern California in 1946 ("Eugenics Pamphlets," 1946) would frequently summarize academic research for their readers. Within issue 48, they discuss Selden Bacon's 1944 article in the *Quarterly Journal of Studies of Alcohol*. Dr. Bacon was a Yale professor who was instrumental in developing approaches that examined alcoholism as a disease rather than simply a genetic failing (Bacon, 1985). Though Bacon carefully points out that alcohol was a "factor of pervasive significance" (Bacon, 1944, p. 125), the pamphlet portrays his work as making alcohol the focus of all shortcomings.

> Over 1,200 arrested inebriates were studied. They seem extraordinarily maladjusted to the marital institution. Only 47% had ever married, whereas 80% of all urban Connecticut males of the same age range were. Of married inebriates, 25% are separated from their wives. Normal expectancy: 4%. In a dozen other categories, the inebriates show their general inferiority".
> ("Eugenics Pamphlets," 1946)

The last word of this quote is quite salient because Bacon's work never equates alcohol and inferiority together. Others took his work and drew their conclusions with it. These conflations exemplify how advocates for eugenics use material to justify their views to make policies like sterilization seem rational.

Eugenicists embrace ideas that "poverty was inbred" (Nourse, 2008, p. 167), dismissing wealth and social circumstances in favor of genetic heritage. "Social inferiority that is permanent and biological – inferiority that is naturalized and thus cannot be overcome – is the hallmark of distinction that are racial in character; it distinguishes them from class distinctions, which are thought to be easily transcended" (Nourse, 2008, p. 167). Poor genetics becomes a justification for sterilization, euthanasia, incarceration, and social isolation. For the United States, some of these concepts are rooted in our very foundational leaders and architects of America. Thomas Jefferson "identified and catalogued apparent racial differences" among his slaves at Monticello (Dorr, 2018, p. 27). He found them inferior and believed their deficiencies were not caused by "their enslaved condition" (Dorr, 2018, p. 27). Gregory Dorr suggests an insidious intellectual balancing act Thomas Jefferson engaged in to justify slavery yet embrace equality.

"Jefferson could espouse the political equality of all men, yet make qualified but invidious distinctions among 'types' of men- and still remain consistent within the framework of natural law and the epistemology of natural philosophy" (Dorr, 2018, pp. 27–28). Simply put, enslaved Blacks were not the same at their core identity, thus not entitled to the same rights. In *Notes on the State of Virginia*, Jefferson compared Augustan Roman Slaves to Virginian ones. "Roman slaves displayed talents as artists, scientists and tutors ... Jefferson found no talent in Virginia" (Cowing, 1971, p. 109). If Jefferson held that enslaved Black people were fundamentally different, then human rights would not apply in the same way. These beliefs are essential to recognizing how American culture recognized the idea of the other from its early years. If we believe we have genetically different others within our society that are lesser, it becomes reasonable to craft a tiered system of inherent rights. It is protectionism at its most significant manifestation. Persons deemed superior have an obligation in this perspective to corral lesser for their good while skirting the fact they developed the rules of the game while acting as its judges. Justifications can also be observed through the entrenched and widespread acceptance of Calvinism across American society regardless of specific faith at the time of the founding.

Calvinism

Ideas of innate superiority and inferiority coupled well with the significant lines of religious thought that dominated early America and helped entrench inequality within their society. American religions of all denominations in the eighteenth century were heavily impacted by Calvinist predestination. According to Hutchinson (2008), approximately 90% of Americans had a Calvinistic religious background rather than a Lutheran one from the Protestant Reformation (pp. 20–21). Furthermore, "the colonists had been at least 85 percent English-speaking Calvinistic Protestants" (Hutchison, 2008, p. 21). According to Gaustad (1952), there were less than six Calvinistic churches in New England in 1740. Within 60 years, there were over 325 Baptist churches, most of which adhered to Calvinistic principles (Gaustad, 1952, p. 43). Without lingering too much on the history of Calvinism within early America, it is essential to highlight how its ideals and values were widespread and engrained within many viewpoints of the citizenry.

One of the ideas central to Calvinism involves predestination. Long before our existence, God had already determined those destined for salvation and damnation. "Calvin explicitly states that God makes his choice regardless of any merit in the subject. Since the decision is made before anyone's birth, it is made beyond the scope of any criterion such as merit or good works" (Cameron, 2003 p. 18). Predestination assigns a person to a fixed state. Condemned sinners were incapable of redemption because the almighty already assigned their fate. Calvinism helps justify inequality while remaining empathic toward others. "The Calvinistic Protestants, of course, made the additional assumption that God's elect were not evenly distributed among the races or over the globe" (Cowing, 1971, p. 98).

These ideas help reconcile ideas about slavery and inferiority within the American colonies and later states. An omniscient and omnipresent God knows all. They make choices about our lives before they even occur. If that same God allows a person to be born into chattel slavery, then it is a choice made by that same deity. Adherents to Calvinist doctrine may not know their ultimate fate but have to place their faith in the grace of God. They live their lives as if they are destined for heaven because to do otherwise would demonstrate a lack of trust in their God.

Similarly, challenging the institution of slavery also runs into the same problem. God had those persons born into slavery. He made those choices before their birth and set their state. From this perspective, anyone challenging slavery also challenges the authority of God. Perfect deities do not make errors. This viewpoint allows many, like Thomas Jefferson, to hold disdain for slavery yet not take steps to abolish it. God gave enslaved people an inferior status, and it is not within our capacity to refute his authority. It also provides a path to square Jefferson's ideas of the inherent inferiority of slaves while still asserting the rights of man. It comes down to your definitions and considerations of who qualifies as a man. In addition, your religious traditions weigh heavily into play. For faiths not imbued with Calvinism, free will would mean something slightly different. Their individual choices factor into their views of personal freedoms and conscience. Calvinism coupled well with maintaining slavery because doing anything else could potentially upend your religiosity. The deep-rooted Calvinism of early America may not have retained its overt framing of religiosity as America grew and developed, but its influences were prevalent.

Eugenics functions as a scientific (pseudoscience) application of Calvinism. Eugenics aims to create the best potential person and society through careful and selective choices. Like Calvinism, many of these choices were already determined before birth by an Almighty. Superiority and inferiority are hard-wired into us, with many eugenicists putting forward ideas that baser instincts drive weaker individuals. They are framed as lesser, with fewer social controls and thoughtful constitutions. Many eugenicists, like Harry Laughlin, argue they are also more fertile than their genetically superior counterparts. Marriage controls, sterilization, isolation, and even removal from the population function as ways to maintain a healthy, superior society. The causes of their supposed lesser status do not matter as much as their actuality. Immigration controls and other preventive measures square with Calvinism because their situation is not questioned. Social welfare and support only provide bandage ornamentation but do not address the root problems within society. They do not solve problems but provide a temporary salve, like a painkiller for a dental cavity. A dentist must tackle decay and drill out a cavity or pull the tooth. Many eugenic points of view align themselves well with early Calvinism. Both also allow for a specific veneer of objectivism, which doubles as a shield. Calvinists cannot question slavery since God allowed persons born as enslaved people. If God objected, no other person would be born in that state. Eugenicists maintain that their goals are to ensure society is healthy, wholesome, and functional.

MUSCULAR CHRISTIANITY AND RACE SUICIDE

One movement whose eugenical connections are often minimized is Muscular Christianity. The Muscular Christianity movement flourished in England and the United States throughout the late nineteenth and early twentieth centuries. While rarely discussed today, we still remember many of its adherents and legacy without including these associations. John Harvey Kellogg, Anthony Drexel Biddle, and Theodore Roosevelt were only some influential men who embraced this movement. Health, patriotism, vigor, 'manliness,' sports, and religiosity blended within Protestant life to form a new masculine ideal. Specifically, adherents stoked fears of "American 'degeneracy'" (Putney, 2001, p. 25), encouraged "virtues of leading a 'strenuous life' replete with exercise" (Putney, 2001, p. 25), and attacked perceptions of a "'feminization' of American Protestantism" (Putney, 2001, p. 25). Historian and advocate Henry C. Mervin attacked "the so-called 'respectable' American, who he termed 'a creature who is what we call oversophisticated and effete'" (Putney, 2001, p. 26). Theodore Roosevelt also claimed that educated and cultured persons looked down upon "rougher and manlier persons, that an advanced state of intellectual development is too often associated with a certain effeminacy of character" (Putney, 2001, p. 26). In other words, modern urbane society for White Protestants turned men into soft characters worthy of disdain. Rugged men without education were thus superior for their strength and unwillingness to turn into sissified dandies. Toughness and rejection of genteel behavior were considered honorable and just. A tough-talking, macho exterior was glorified as true and righteous. Exercise and the outdoors were remedies to weaknesses created by modern life. The most famous organization spawned by this movement was the Young Men's Christian Organization, or the YMCA, which stressed the importance of athleticism in daily life. These ideas fed into deep-seated nativist perspectives that held "the United States should be preserved for the Anglo-Saxon race, Protestant faith, and traditional American values" (Engs, 2005, p. 155).

The connections between eugenics and Muscular Christianity are deep and well-rooted. Eugenicists considered physical training moral and demanded its implementation in public schools (Putney, 2001, p. 38). Masculinity, race, and fitness were blended into a new model for good White Protestant Americans. Edward Ross (1901) was the very first to use the term 'race suicide' when he claimed lower fertility rates among 'good'

Whites (he intentionally excluded Irish and French Canadians) allowed weaker, more fertile immigrant groups to swamp American culture with inadequate stock and values. Theodore Roosevelt spoke regularly about his concerns of 'race suicide' with his first usage in a foreword for a book where he bemoaned men or women who did not marry as a "criminal against race" (Van Vorst & Van Vorst, 1903). Roosevelt also believed White Protestant women who did not have children were likewise the same because they were contributing to the death of their genetic line and ancestry. Theodore Roosevelt had strident views about race suicide and felt White Americans needed to have children for the health of the nation. Myre St. Wald Iseman (1912) wrote a book entitled *Race Suicide*, which examined race worldwide, with several chapters devoted to the United States. Regions have characteristics drawn from assumptions about their immigration patterns. Abortion was openly discussed as abhorrent and inappropriate for wealthier groups (Rentoul, 1906, p. 105), with sterilization as a preferable option. Abortions among the wealthy removed potential high-value White citizenry. It was not about an overarching concern for general humanity at this time. The late nineteenth and early twentieth centuries saw a spate of authors in the United States and Great Britain bemoaning the state of society. They saw the world awash with "physical deterioration and of mental degeneration" (Rentoul, 1906, p. 2). The advocacy of government intervention sprung from the general annoyance of their perceived failures of the current system. "At present we are engaged in the apparently pleasant pastime of manufacturing diseased infants, idiots, imbeciles, and insane. We allow all these to marry and beget offspring. ... The cowardly practice of *laissez faire* has been tried and has been found wanting" (Rentoul, 1906, p. 2). They frequently used loaded language to justify their concerns. For example, Rentoul (1906) referred to people "suffering from mental and physical disease – the scum and flotsam" (p. 3). These persons themselves were not the problem, but instead, the system that allowed for their creation. Rentoul was firmly against the marriage of White citizens and foreigners, going as far as to say, "A few of us know the terrible monstrosities produced by the intermarriage of the white man and black, the white man with the redskin, the white man with the native Hindu, or the white man with the Chinese" (Rentoul, 1906, pp. 4–5). The naturalization of foreigners meant national racial stereotypes would no longer be accurate.

The term 'race suicide' became somewhat of a buzzword of the period. Whites worried about destroying Anglo-Saxon roots and values by choosing smaller families and being outpaced by immigrant communities. Many people within the time espoused virtues that blended healthy living and bountiful White American Protestant families that could weather the forces of social dilution caused by immigration. While mostly remembered for cereal today, John Harvey Kellogg was integral to this movement. He founded the Battle Creek Sanitarium, where he advocated exercise, vegetarianism, and various physical therapies to improve general well-being. In Battle Creek, Michigan, Kellogg, and other prominent eugenicists founded the Race Betterment Foundation. They were primarily concerned with promoting hygiene, exercise, and sound Christian living to curb threats created by race mixing and the mentally unfit.

> What the world needs at the present time more than anything else is race improvement. If race degeneracy is to be arrested, it will only be accomplished by the development of a more resistant and better type of men-a tougher, more enduring man more capable of wrestling successfully with the problems of the twentieth century and the greater centuries to come. (Kellogg, 1914, p. 663)

Eugenics in Mainstream

While many of these ideas and ideals are outdated, their importance is often overlooked and underplayed within modern academia and broader culture. In the early twentieth century, these beliefs were considered mainstream and scientifically accurate to middle- and upper-class Protestant Whites. They reinforced their prejudices in ways that justified them and validated their fears of the other. In many ways, it allowed them to champion empathy while simultaneously endorsing sterilization and restricting immigration with claims of the greater good for all. These beliefs are factual, not just opinions in their view. Thus, any measures taken to advocate them were considered proper and appropriate.

They used terms like defective, unfit, and insane to describe specific characteristics and then pointed toward genetic inheritance as the origin of these concerns. Eugenicists were concerned with public health and improving the circumstances for people within their society. Crime was believed to be hereditary (Thomson, 1870), and by the early twentieth century, racial attributes were considered part of eugenic research (Roberts, 1908; Woodworth, 1910). Robert Woodworth (1910) argued that only the best individuals should be selected when considering those immigrating to new countries. Others ("A Plea," 1907) complain about the societal cost when "the defect in question is mainly due to congenital weakness" (pp. 123–124) and maintaining permanent segregation is the only solution. Johnson (1909) contended restrictive marriage laws, sterilization, and euthanasia were not practical and instead pushed for the segregation of immigrants and genetic undesirables in secluded colony institutional farms. Crane (1909) discusses how many American states in 1908 banned marriage for people with epilepsy, the feeble-minded, sufferers of syphilis or gonorrhea, first cousins, as well as the insane. By 1907, Indiana allowed sterilization of persons convicted of a felony three times as well as any "idiots, rapists, and imbeciles" (Crane, 1909, p. 122) if a board determined them to be 'unimprovable.' Likewise, in "Maine, Michigan, Wisconsin and Arizona all marriages become void without a decree" (Crane, 1909, p. 122) if an undesirable person could not be rehabilitated to a board's satisfaction. States were legally allowed to invalidate marriages if they found the persons who entered into them to be not to their liking and undesirable. These ideas persisted throughout the first half of the twentieth century. Horsley (1944) referred to America when he stated "we are largely breeding from the runts" (p. 93), and groups with less than desirable traits were overpopulating us. Horsley wanted more stringent controls on reproduction stating "If the candidates for marriage are moronic or psychotic or if they come from markedly moronic or psychotic families, the marriage license should either be refused or it should be granted only if the applicants are sterilized" (Horsley, 1944, p. 94). Orebaugh (1929) asserted that America was weakening "due to a degeneration of the national stock resulting from its intermixture with disharmonic and inferior races" (p. vi). For eugenic advocates, the foundations of American society were at risk. Our country was under siege from immigration, with all of our long-standing populations rebranded away from their roots and recast as wholesome, earnest immigrants in the image of Mayflower, not Moll Flanders.

Fitter Family & Better Baby Contests

Eugenics advocates within American society in the early twentieth century wanted to help cultivate the best exemplars of our people. These aspirations embraced aspects that smack heavily of social engineering. Families were examined like cattle at fairs to highlight who was considered the idealized American. Fairs, state or local, were places where communities came together to show off their best wares. Many people spend all year cultivating the perfect farm animals, tweaking their best recipes, or raising the ideal vegetable examples for these events. 'Fitter Family,' and 'Better Baby' contests are set alongside livestock and farming competitions in fairs during the early twentieth century. Fitter family and baby contests were intentionally held at agricultural fairs. "Fitter family contests appealed to a deeply rooted sense of nostalgia for the rural family at a time when the nation was becoming increasing urban, when rural children were choosing not to stay on the farm, and when the culture of the Roaring Twenties challenged 'traditional values'" (Lovett, 2007, pp. 70–71). These events matter because they were developed and organized by groups and persons who believed eugenics was the best path forward. In Indiana, there were concerted attempts to "control procreation and endorsed only the birth of the 'best' and healthiest babies" (Stern, 2002, p. 743). This state passed the nation's first sterilization laws on eugenics grounds (Stern, 2002). From 1920 to 1932, Indiana had extremely popular Better Babies contests at their annual state fair, though the origin of such events was the 1911 Iowa State Fair (Stern, 2002, p. 748). Louisiana has, at times, claimed to have originated them in 1908 (Stern, 2002, note 60, p. 752), but it is incontrovertible they developed in the first two decades of the twentieth century. These "eugenics exhibits at state fairs helped garner public support for social reforms such as immigration restrictions, marriage restrictions, euthanasia, segregation, and compulsory institutionalization and sterilization of those deemed degenerates or defectives" (Rubenstein, 2009, p. 179). Dr. Ada E Schweizer, the person who developed Indiana's contests, stated, "You can not make a silk purse out of a sow's ear, neither can we make a citizen out of an idiot or any person who is not well born" (Stern, 2002, p. 749).

Mary T. Watts, who was involved in the implementation of many of these fitter family and baby contests, stated,

> When someone asks about what it is all about, we say, 'While the stock judges are testing Holsteins, Jerseys, and Whitefaces in the stock pavilion, we are judging the Joneses, Smiths, and the Johnsons,' and nearly every one replies: 'I think it is about time people had a little of the attention that is given to animals'. (Rydell, 1993, pp. 49-50)

Watts gave eugenics a relatable analogy many people could understand. With audiences composed of state fair dwellers, these comparisons were reasonable and likely more comprehendible than an academic discussing genetics conceptually. In addition, most farmers understood the importance of castrating or putting down bulls to avoid overpopulation and selectively breeding livestock to enhance the most desirable traits within their animals. From this perspective, eugenics extends ideas already prevalent on farms and turns them toward humans. Fairs that also had sideshows with exhibitions of often genetically divergent persons, fitter families, and better babies played upon fears of the different. Parents wanted their children to be the ideal and worthy in the eyes of society.

Furthermore, legal restrictions toward 'unfit' people, be it immigration, sterilization, or miscegenation laws to prohibit them, are not unreasonable when framed as if you are managing livestock for a farm. The infringement of others' personal rights and choices balances against their fears of their stock weakening. Advocates of eugenics played into these agricultural perceptions to emphasize reasonableness and make it sound less of an invasive attack upon basic human rights. It is also easier to draw these conclusions in the broad abstract as policy rather than as individual choices. Once their children or families pass a bar and are considered worthy, their achievement needs to be preserved and extended. The best baby or fittest family needs to get stronger over time, not weaker. Challengers (e.g., other ethnic or racial groups) are not framed empathically, but more as a zero-sum game where there always must exist winners and losers. If the strongest survive a Darwinist battle, those considered the 'fittest' will seek to prune the weaker branches.

The 1925 Indiana State Fair brochure sets out the awards and prizes for the babies. "The Indianapolis News will give $10 in gold and a beautiful cup to the first baby in each section of each division" ("Indiana," p. 213). Divisions were broken down by sex and age. Twelve to twenty-four months was in one category, while twenty-four to thirty-six in another. Twins and triplets each had separate categories and a championship prize for the best boy and best girl baby across all classes. Furthermore, "One hundred dollars will be divided between all babies who have scores of 995 or better out of a possible 1000 points who have not won any of the foregoing prizes" ("Indiana," p. 214). Children were scored similarly to livestock and also scored by county representation. In addition, "every baby examined at the State Fair this year and last becomes a member of the State Fair Health Club, as his parents promise to follow health advice of examining physicians" ("Indiana," p. 212).

Sideshows as Object Lessons

These displays of graded and idealized persons must be remembered in the context where they were shown. Fairs often included livestock displays, convention hall exhibitions, and the midway. The midway frequently had entertainment, rides, and sideshows. Circus and wrestling acts evolved next to sideshow entertainment. Circus often had animals and entertainers showing the fantastical. Wrestling, at this time, displayed choreographed fits of strength with characters playing up antagonisms for the crowd. The audience is encouraged to cheer, jeer, and vent their spleens in a curated show for their entertainment. Other parts of the sideshow contained the freak and geek shows. Geek shows, by definition, are persons who have specialized skills or body modification that are outside the generalized mainstream of society.

For example, swallowing swords falls into a geek act because the average person would likely impale themselves if they attempted it without training. On the other hand, freak shows are more salient within the context of eugenics and this social period of American life. These sorts of shows focused on genetic outliers, mutations, recessive traits, or other afflictions that differed from conventional or dominant ones. People would line up and pay to sit and watch a show or walk through an exhibition with persons on display. One of the real cruxes of these acts involved compensation. For many, the pay in these shows was superior to anything they could earn in traditional employment. Disability supports were non-existent at this time, and circus allowed people to earn an often decent living, though they had to accept being gawked at as a morality lesson. During this late nineteenth to early twentieth century period, at the height of eugenics, people would be shown for the otherness. This separateness extended to persons of different races and cultures as well. It was not unheard of to see persons mimicking various tribal groups worldwide. These acts primarily functioned as ways to make people feel better about their own lives. Freak shows of persons on display with physical deformities must be remembered as exhibitions that were on the same grounds as ones that commended the 'fittest' or best genetic families. These were also frequently near tribal persons on display, be they Native American, African, Inuit, Aboriginal, or others. Each spectacle served as educational purposes for a society steeped in eugenic perspectives. They reinforced ideas of inherent White European superiority. They also served as object lessons about the perils of 'poor breeding.' Eugenics preaches the 'good breeding' doctrine that produces superior stock within society. These presentations buffered their claims through exoticism, voyeurism, and, bluntly, gawking to highlight what happens when people do not reproduce with diligence and care. The persons on display were not curiosities of genetic diversity, underscoring the depth and breadth of the human experience. Instead, they traded on fearmongering to help create social and political support for isolation from the other. Eugenicists advocated for sterilization of the exact types of persons on display in these exhibitions. In a real sense, eugenicists and their political allies benefitted from the outrage that would, at times, follow these types of presentations. Sterilization, as a way to contain and inhibit these traits within future generations, would appear more thoughtful, reasonable, and not an overstep of personal rights. In many ways, people at the freak shows were superficial displays with no insight into their interior lives. Performers often and frequently did live dignified lives off-stage and off-season, but the audiences could care less about them at those times. Audiences looked at them and came to their conclusions without any insight into them as actual persons. They functioned as object lessons to highlight hyperbolic rationales for sterilization as well as immigration restrictions lest 'these' people mainstream and challenge the norms of their ordered culture.

Framing the Outdoors as Healthy to Contrast with Urban Immigration

It also fits within the general attitudes of American society. "At the turn of the century, a back-to-nature movement, built on a romanticized version of nature and rural environments, swept the country. Boy Scouts, Campfire Girls, Woodcraft Indians, and several other organizations sought to expose children to healthy influence of nature study" (Judd & Hinze, 2023, p. 183). Political machines, heavy immigration into cities, and often inadequate municipal services made many people frustrated with urban areas. Nature became a refuge as well as a whole thing. Leisure hunting greatly expanded at this time as people began to engage in the activity of being part of nature rather than simply getting food for survival. The general idea of country clubs grew tremendously in this period as well. Their very name implies the ideal embedded within their existence. People sought to be part of nature, albeit a curated and carefully prescribed version. Nostalgia for simpler times and general unhappiness with urban society intermingle in ways that helped prime the population for these eugenic appeals. Americans increasingly framed rural America as an idealized place where our most wholesome and best originate. Those attitudes craft a protectionist frame around the nation. Generally speaking, protectionism occurs when rights or actions are restricted to avoid harm, often unintentionally caused by themselves. Restriction of a woman's right to vote was frequently framed in a protectionist lens before the attainment of suffrage. It was commonplace to hear that women were too delicate for the combative world of politics. Denying them the right to vote was for their safety or welfare. William T. Sedgwick, in an extended piece, explains male and female biological differences and how they are suitable for different tasks. He used barnyard examples to highlight the difference between cows and bulls within the role of a farm. The piece largely bemoans attempts at women's voting as a pretense for a feminist movement. While asserting his subject matter is neutral, he claims "there is a great mental difference between the sexes" (MacAdam, 1914, p. 30) and finds women lacking capability.

Eugenic appeals, in other words, play upon these rural sympathies, changing societies, and dissatisfaction with urban realities to create atmospheres at these fairs where overwhelmingly White nuclear families are revered as the gold standard. Their children are seen as the hope for future societies. As a result, these precious fitter family baby's futures must be protected against unwholesome influences. Normative judgments become cloaked within empirical data, like head width, height, and weight. Biased, non-random samples of populations are portrayed as the best exemplars by experts. In a more scientific sense, these attempts fit within the framework of what is often referred to as 'positive eugenics,' where people deemed fit are encouraged "to reproduce often and responsibly, with an awareness of their own heredity and that of their prospective mates" (Boudreau, 2005, p. 367). Larger 'fit' families coupled with sterilization and restrictive immigration would help preserve the quality of the nation.

Eugenics Turns to Immigration Policy

Around 1910, we saw a shifting focus in American eugenics toward concerns about immigration. Robert DeCourcy Ward (1910) asserted we are forming a 'new race' in our country and need to be careful in the "selection of the fathers and mothers of future American children through our power to regulate alien immigration" (p. 57). He continues by stating, "we have allowed Europe, and even Asia and Africa, to throw every sort of material, while we ourselves have been blissfully – shall we not rather say criminally?- careless as to what the final product is to be" (Ward, 1910, 57–58). Ward is quite blunt in his assessments. His frankness helps us understand these positions better without the euphemistic language many of his contemporaries use to couch their arguments. "National eugenics means the prevention of the breeding of the unfit native, no less than the prevention of the admission, and of the breeding after admission, of the unfit alien" (Ward, 1910, pp. 63–64). The determination of unfit, however, lies with the eye of the beholder. He concluded with a call for protecting America from the immigrants who "George William Curtis called that 'watering of the nation's life-blood' which results from their breeding after admission" (Ward, 1910, p. 67). The overarching goal of eugenics involves controlling who is allowed to develop ancestral roots within a society. Immigration restrictions are one way, but limitations upon procreation are another. Inferiority was often used as a basis for sterilization. "Almost three-quarters of the women sterilized in the California program, the country's largest by far, were labeled sexual deviates or prostitutes" (Nourse, 2008, p. 61). Immorality was "ascribed to their blood, and then once there, circled back to confirm the diagnosis of a weak mind" (Nourse, 2008, p. 61).

Early twentieth-century American and British thought leaders had deep concerns over the composition of their societies. As the twentieth century progressed, containment of genetic stock became the dominant idea. The Second International Congress was held at the American National History Museum in New York City in 1921. The Darwin and Forestry Halls in the museum were converted to Eugenics Hall. This exhibition was created by a $2500 gift from Mary Williamson Averell Harriman, who founded the Eugenics Record Office (Laughlin, 1923, p. 13). They had many presentations on a wide variety of topics. The United States Bureau of the Census was an exhibitor with a display entitled "Comparative Fecundity of Different Racial Stocks in the United States. Predominance of Foreign Stock" (Laughlin, 1923, p. 26). E.J. Lidbetter, a "civil service bureaucrat in the London City Council's poor law authority (Chase, 1977, p. 281), gave a presentation entitled "Pedigrees of Pauper Stocks." He wrote a summary at the end of his paper where he found an "existence of a definite race of chronic pauper stocks" (Lidbetter, 1923, p. 397).

He also found "modern methods of public and private charity tend to encourage the increase of this class by relieving parents of the normal responsibility of parenthood" (Lidbetter, 1923, p. 397). He concludes the paper with "the reduction of this class may be brought about by a due observance of the laws of heredity, so far as they are surely known, and that the reduction may become progressive in proportion as our knowledge grows" (Lidbetter, 1923, p. 397). A permanent poor class exists within society; more importantly, social welfare does not work. Social support does more harm than good because parents pass off accountability, allowing this group to grow unchecked. His last statement implies careful breeding needs to be employed until better options present themselves. The phrasing of reduction is broad enough to encompass restricting marriages and childbirth in a wide variety of ways, but most likely sterilization and careful mate selection.

The Impact Harry H. Laughlin

By the 1920s, one of the leading forces behind these policies was Harry H. Laughlin. In 1922, he published *Eugenical Sterilization in the United States*, whose impact permanently shaped the world.

> Dr. Laughlin persistently insisted high American living standards meant admission was equivalent to the gift to the immigration of a fortune. He declared that none should be allowed entrance here unless they could definitely prove their eugenic worth was greater than the American average. ("Eugenics Pamphlets," 1946)

Laughlin testified in front of Congress supporting the 1924 Immigration Acts, which eventually implemented country quotas for admission. During his November 21, 1922 testimony, when discussing inadequate immigrants, he said, "Some of our finest and most desirable immigrants from Norway" (Laughlin, 1922a, p. 755). He went on to say, "The United States must differentiate sharply between a political asylum for the high minded and splendidly equipped but much oppressed patriots, on one hand, and a custodial asylum for degenerates, on the other" (Laughlin, 1922a, p. 757). Laughlin advocated for the use of deportation to keep undesirable people out. He asserted deportation "is the last line of defense in our national nettle against undesirable alien qualities"

(Laughlin, 1922a, p. 758). He was concerned about their genetic contribution to the United States, not their physical presence. He is unequivocal in this regard because he views immigration as "essentially and fundamentally a racial and biological problem. There are many factors to consider, but, from the standpoint of the future, immigration is primarily a long time national investment in human family stocks" (Laughlin, 1922a, p. 759).

His book was instrumental in 18 states passing legislation based on his proposals, the most infamous being the Virginia Sterilization Act of 1924. Aside from being held as constitutional by the U.S. Supreme Court in *Buck v. Bell* (1927), these Laughlin laws were the model for the *Law for the Prevention of Hereditarily Diseased Offspring (Gesetz zur Verhütung erbkranken Nachwuchses)* implemented by the German Reichstag in 1933. Laughlin was later given an "honorary Doctorate of Medicine from the University of Heidelberg in Germany" in 1936 for his work on sterilization of unfit populations ("Harry Laughlin," 2021). The impact of Laughlin cannot be underemphasized. Accolades given to his work legitimized it and created a gravitas for the validity and implementation of his eugenic-based findings.

Why Does It Still Matter?

American eugenics exists not just as an odd curiosity of our nation's past but rather as a sweeping movement that helped change the world's fate. These policies were broad, mainstream, and fully integral in American life. They were accepted, especially by those of healthy Northern European Protestant descent, as confirmation of their innate superiority. "By 1928, eugenics was a topic in 376 separate college courses, which enrolled approximately 20,000 students. A content analysis of high school science text books published between 1914 and 1948 indicates that a majority presented eugenics was a legitimate science" (Selden, n.d.). Pauly (1991) points out eugenics became part of high school textbooks in 1914, but in college texts such as Michael Guyer's *Being Well-Born*, treatment was "perfunctory, narrowly focused on specific medical defects" (p. 687) instead of more significant issues like racial hygiene. Guyer's textbook advocated for "a conscious attempt to breed a superior race... and the elimination of the obviously unfit by preventing their reproduction" (Guyer, 1916, p. 301). Eugenical ideas were not a passing fancy, but rather, a grounding worldview that spanned over half a century. While it may have peaked in the 1920s and 1930s, the foundation was already present long before that time. At its heart, American eugenic policy centered itself around eliminating undesirable traits determined by the dominant social forces. These primarily manifested as genetic defects (which often included poverty) and racial and ethnic deviations from White Christian Europeans. Miscegenation laws and immigration restrictions were fundamental to American policy to preserve presumed Northern European racial integrity. Eugenics advocate and physician Joseph DeJarnette believed forced sterilization was the only way to improve the racial stock of Virginia. "In 1934 he implored the General Assembly to broaden the scope of Virginia's sterilization law; 'the Germans,' he complained, 'are beating us at our own game and are more progressive than we are.' DeJarnette never wavered in his advocacy of eugenics, not even after the revelation of the Nazi Holocaust" (Dorr, 2021). Widespread acceptance of eugenics only faded from broad popularity as the 'enthusiastic' implementation of Nazi Germany's extermination policies became more well-known and scientific research grew more rigorous. However, generations of Americans were educated and lived under a system that presented these ideas as facts fully integrated into daily life.

When groups within a society want to complain about changing demographics, immigration policies have long been an easy target. Donald Trump has referred to other immigrants with phrases like "so many criminals being dumped" along with immigrants "poisoning the blood" of the United States (LeVine & Sacchetti, 2023). This language echoes advocates of restrictions who were concerned about race suicide in the early twentieth century. Writing about immigration into Great Britain, Rentoul (1906) pointed out that by accepting aliens, "England can be made the dumping ground of other nations so that the latter may get rid of their undesirable class" (p. 104). He later went on to call for compulsory sterilization of "all idiots, imbeciles, feeble-minded, epileptics, lunatics, deaf-mutes, defective and backward children, habitual inebriates, habitual vagrants, public prostitutes, many sexual perverts, and markedly neurotic persons" (Rentoul, 1906, p. 145). Eugenic beliefs on immigration, intelligence, and reproduction all still have impacts on our world today. Stern (2005) points out Lewis Terman's book, *The Measurement of Intelligence*, was integral in formulating the 1924 Johnson-Reed Immigration Act because they heavily relied upon his scales to determine thresholds for low IQs (p. 19). These scales were also utilized when gauging compulsory sterilization levels for feeble-mindedness (Stern, 2005, p. 19). Terman (1916), in his work, strongly insinuates feeble-mindedness tied to negative social traits. He states, "not all criminals are feeble-minded, but all feeble-minded are at least potential criminals. That every feeble-minded woman is a potential prostitute would hardly be disputed by any one. ... Morality cannot flower and fruit if intelligence remains infantile" (p. 11).

Eugenics attempted to give Whites of Anglo-Saxon ancestry a path toward greatness through a road map paved with confirmation bias. Science gave prejudice a way to create a veneer of objectivity while embracing normative favoritism every step of the way. In short, they made a rigged game. Specific individuals within other ethnic or racial groups could be considered outstanding examples yet still be framed as outliers. Eugenics gave prejudiced attitudes means to have it both ways. They can exclude most while embracing those select few without confronting their inherent bigotry. Immigration restrictions, quotas, asylums, and other barriers were all about sex. They were never about infrastructural strains on the population. Instead, they felt the only proper way to prevent procreation was through the ultimate barrier method. Spatial segregation, sterilization, and physical separation were the only ways to ensure genetic integrity. Immigration walls are less about job protection and more about making sure the country does not turn into a promiscuous trollop that allows anyone to breed inside her borders.

REFERENCES

A Plea for the Mentally Defective. (1907). *Charity Organisation Review*, 21(123), 120–131.

Bacon, S. D. (1944). Inebriety, Social Integration, and Marriage. *Quarterly Journal of Studies of Alcohol*, 5(1), 86–125.

Bacon, S. D. (1985). Conversation with Selden D. Bacon. *British Journal of Addiction*, 80(2), 115–120.

Boudreau, E. B. (2005). "Yea, I Have a Goodly Heritage": Health Versus Heredity in the Fitter Family Contests, 1920–1928. *Journal of Family History*, 30(4), 366–387.

Brown, M. J. (1935). *An Introduction to Eugenics*. Chapman & Grimes.

Cameron, K. (2003). Sovereignty of the Perverse: Democratic Subjectivity and Calvin's Doctrine of Predestination. *Literature and Psychology*, 49, 16–44.

Chase, A. (1977). *The Legacy of Malthus: The Social Costs of the New Scientific Racism*. Random House.

Cowing, C. B. (1971). *The Great Awakening and the American Revolution: Colonial Thought in the 18th Century*. Rand McNally & Co.
Crane, R. N. (1909). Experiments in Eugenics by American State Legislatures. *Journal of the Society of Comparative Legislation, 10*(1), 120–122.
Darwin, C. (1859). *On the Origin of Species by Means of National Selection, or the Preservation of Favoured Races in the Struggle for Life*. John Murray.
Davies, J. L., & Vaughan, D. J. (1935). *The Republic of Plato*. Macmillan and Co.
Dorr, G. M. (2018). *Segregation's Science: Eugenics and Society in Virginia*. University of Virginia Press.
Dorr, G. M. (2021). DeJarnette, Joseph S. (1866–1957). In *Encyclopedia Virginia*. https://encyclopediavirginia.org/entries/dejarnette-joseph-s-1866-1957
Elderton, E. M. (1910). *A First Study of the Influence of Parental Alcoholism on the Physique and Ability of Offspring*. Dulau and Company.
Engs, R. (2005). *The Eugenics Movement: An Encyclopedia*. Greenwood Press.
Eugenics Pamphlets. (1946). *Eugenics Society of Northern California* [Brochure].
Fetal Alcohol Spectrum Disorders. (n.d.). Centers for Disease Control and Prevention. https://www.cdc.gov/ncbddd/fasd/index.html
Galton, M. (1883). *Inquiries into Human Faculty and its Development*. Macmillan and Co.
Gaustad, E. S. (1952). Baptists and the Great Awakening. *The Chronicle, XV*, 41–48.
Guyer, M. F. (1916). *Being Well-Born, an Introduction to Eugenics*. The Bobbs-Merrill Company Publishers.
Harry Laughlin and Eugenics. (2021). *A Selection of Objects from Harry H. Laughlin Papers, Truman State University*. https://historyofeugenics.truman.edu/exchanging-ideas/international-discourse/nazi-connection/
Heron, David. (1907). *A First Study of the Statistics of Insanity and the Inheritance of the Insane Diathesis*. Francis Galton Laboratory of National Eugenics.
Horsley, J. S. (1944). Breeding Better People for Peace: Human Nature Can Be Changed. *Virginia Medical Monthly, 71*, 93–95.
Howard, G. E. (1910). Alcoholism and Crime. *American Journal of Sociology, XXIV*, 6.
Hutchison, W. R. (2008). *Religious Pluralism in America: The Contentious History of a Founding Ideal*. Yale University Press.
Indiana State Fair. (1925). *State Fair Program* [Brochure]. https://indianamemory.contentdm.oclc.org/digital/collection/ISFEC/id/9054
Iseman, M. S. W. (1912). *Race Suicide*. The Cosmopolitan Press.
Jefferson, T. (1832). *Notes on the State of Virginia*. Lilly and Wait.

Johnson, A. (1909). Race Improvement by Control of Defectives (Negative Eugenics). *The Annals of American Academy of Political and Social Science*, *34*(1), 22–29.
Judd, D. R., & Hinze, A. M. (2023). *City Politics: The Political Economy of Urban America* (11th ed.). Routledge.
Kellogg, J. H. (1914). Relation of Public Health to Race Degeneracy. *American Journal of Public Health*, *4*(8), 649–663.
Laughlin, H. H. (1923). *The Second International Exhibition of Eugenics*. Williams & Wilkins Company.
Laughlin, H. H. (1922a, November 21). Analysis of America's Modern Melting Pot. Remarks in Hearings Before the House Committee on Immigration and Naturalization. Sixty-Seventh Congress, Third session.
Laughlin, H. H. (1922b). *Eugenical Sterilization in the United States*. Psychopathic Laboratory of the Municipal Court of Chicago.
LeVine, M., & Sacchetti, M. (2023, December 18). Trump Reprises Dehumanizing Language on Undocumented Immigrants, Warns of Invasion. *The Washington Post*. https://www.washingtonpost.com/politics/2023/12/18/trump-immigrants-invasion-dehumanizing/
Lidbetter, E. L. (1923). Pedigree of Pauper Stocks. In *Eugenics, Genetics and the Family, Vol. I, Scientific Papers of the Second International Congress of Eugenics* (pp. 392–397). Williams & Wilkins Company.
Lovett, L. L. (2007). Fitter Families for Future Firesides: Florence Sherbon and Popular Eugenics. *The Public Historian*, *29*(3), 69–85.
MacAdam, G. (1914, January 18). Feminist Revolutionary Principle Is Biological Bosh. *The New York Times*, p. 30.
Mayo Clinic Staff. (2018, January 10). Fetal Alcohol Syndrome. *Mayo Clinic*. https://www.mayoclinic.org/diseases-conditions/fetal-alcohol-syndrome/symptoms-causes/syc-20352901
Medico-Psychological Association of Great Britain and Ireland. (1906). *The British Medical Journal*, *2*(2379), 259–260.
Nourse, V. F. (2008). *In Reckless Hands: Skinner v. Oklahoma and the Near-Triumph of American Eugenics*. Norton.
Orebaugh, D. A. (1929). *Crime, Degeneracy and Immigration: Their Interrelations and Interreactions*. R.G. Badger.
Pauly, P. J. (1991). The Development of High School Biology: New York City, 1900–1925. *Isis*, *82*(4), 662–688.
Pearson, K. (1912). *The Groundwork of Eugenics*. Cambridge University Press.
Pearson, K., & Elderton, E. M. (1910). *A Second Study of the Influence of Parental Alcoholism on the Physique and Ability of the Offspring: Being a Reply to Certain Medical Critics of the First Memoir and an Examination of the Rebutting Evidence*. Dulau and Company.

Putney, C. (2001). *Muscular Christianity: Manhood and Sports in Protestant America, 1880–1920*. Harvard University Press.
Rentoul, R. R. (1906). *Race Culture; or, Race Suicide: (A Plea for the Unborn)*. The Walter Scott Publishing Co.
Roberts, W. J. (1908). Review: The Racial Interpretation of History and Politics. *International Journal of Ethics, 18*(4), 475–492.
Ross, E. A. (1901). The Causes of Race Superiority. *Annals of the Institute for Political Science, 18*, 67–89.
Rubenstein, A. (2009). Pumpkins, Pigs, and People. *Nursing History Review, 17*, 179–184. https://doi.org/10.1891/1062-8061.17.179
Rydell, R. W. (1993). *World of Fairs: The Century-of-Progress Expositions*. The University of Chicago Press.
Selden, Steve. (n.d.). Eugenics Popularization. *Image Archive on the American Eugenics Movement*. http://www.eugenicsarchive.org/html/eugenics/essay6text.html
Stern, A. M. (2002). Making Better Babies: Public Health and Race Betterment in Indiana, 1920–1935. *American Journal of Public Health, 92*(5), 742–752.
Stern, A. M. (2005). *Eugenic Nation: Faults and Frontiers of Better Breeding in Modern America* (2nd ed.). University of California Press.
Terman, L. (1916). *The Measurement of Intelligence: An Explanation of and a Complete Guide for the Use of the Stanford Revision and Extension of the Binet-Simon Intelligence Scale*. Houghton Mifflin Company.
Thomson, J. B. (1870). *The Hereditary Nature of Crime*. Geo. P. Bacon.
Van Vorst, J., & Van Vorst, M. (1903). *The Woman Who Toils: Being the Experiences of Two Gentlewomen as Factory Girls*. Doubleday.
Ward, R. D. (1910). National Eugenics in Relation to Immigration. *The North American Review, 192*(656), 56–67.
Woodworth, R. S. (1910). Racial Differences in Mental Traits. *Science, 31*(788), 171–186.

CHAPTER 2

Mammy Statues, Power, and the Importance of Framing

Abstract Faithful slave statuary was popularized in the late nineteenth and early twentieth centuries. This chapter explores how these statues were often linked to political power and participation. Statues to honor mammies were often framed in the same breath as withholding minority suffrage rights. Mammy statues provided physical representations of accepted and idealized behaviors and paths for persons of color. The chapter explores how expectations of behavior reinforce power dynamics. This chapter discusses the several faithful slave memorials leading up to the attempt to authorize one in Washington, D.C. It also outlines how the bill for this statue overlapped with testimony about immigration restrictions and eugenics displays in Congress.

Keywords Mammy statue · Eugenics · Faithful slave · Heflin · Confederate memorials

People tend to accept what is presented to them as the truth. We perceive things as 'always been there' because they have been so during our lifetime. However, it does not mean that perspective is wholly accurate. Statuary allows us to create a physical representation of things valued by a society. Many monuments and statues exist as a way to remember people or events across the passage of time. These tributes are not objective and endure as normative interpretations from a specific moment in history. Many assume these effigies are impartial, but they are creations of their times. Choices of what is remembered, how it is depicted, and who is represented all give us insight into the values meant to be passed on through memorials.

In the early twentieth century, there existed a moment where the United States was interested in building monuments to Southern Mammys (Mammies). Mammies were house slaves tasked with rearing their master's children on a plantation. They were sometimes wet nurses, cooks, nannies, governesses, and any other duties that involved the care of the youngsters. They were enslaved but frequently referred to as trusted and loyal household members. Most depictions of mammies show them using pidgin English. The most well-known mammies are Mammy, portrayed by Hattie McDaniel in *Gone with the Wind* (1939), and Aunt Jemima, a popular image on pancake batter. Hattie McDaniel won an Academy Award in 1939 for her portrayal of Mammy in *Gone with the Wind*. Her depiction has become the framework for all future assumptions about how a mammy should appear in American life.

The movement to build statues builds upon itself in ways that reflect the politics of that moment in American history. Faithful slaves are seen as simple, loyal servants who devote their lives to their employers. These statues, however, exist with a more complex reality, borne from a desire to fondly remember halcyon days to help forward one politician's political ambitions. It later gains ground through the political mechanizations of others in different ways.

Robert Love Taylor

The story of Confederate monuments, mammy statues, and historical memory is somewhat complex and convoluted. One of the earliest starting points for the groundswell of monument support seems intertwined with Robert Love Taylor, his life, and his livelihood. Robert Love Taylor, or 'Our Bob,' was born in Happy Valley, Tennessee. His family moved to New Jersey, about 20 miles east of Philadelphia, during the Civil War because of the occupation of the Confederate Army in East Tennessee (Augsburg, 1925, p. 27). His family returned to their home state after the war. He and his brother, Alfred, were key figures in Tennessee politics in the late nineteenth and early twentieth centuries. Robert was in the U.S.

House of Representatives from 1879–1881, Governor of Tennessee from 1887–1891, 1897–1999, and U.S. Senator from 1907 until he died in 1912. Though Taylor is more of a historical footnote now, he was extremely popular in his day. The brothers, though close to each other, aligned with different political parties. Both men were pitted against each other in the Tennessee 1886 gubernatorial race. The assumption was that the Republican Party ran Alfred to drive Robert out of the race. The election was referred to as the 'War of the Roses,' intentionally drawing a comparison to English history, in which the Yorks and Lancasters were pitted against each other. One side aligned with red roses in that conflict, while the other was white. "Republican stalwarts wore a red one in their buttonholes; followers of Bob flaunted the white" (Augsburg, 1925, p. 52). The men traveled together on the campaign, and on at least one occasion, Bob accidentally gave a speech written for Alfred (Augsburg, 1925, p. 54).

Both men were skilled and vibrant orators. This talent did not extend into their professional lives. Each found themselves financially strapped after serving terms in different levels of government. Robert Taylor was so broke financially "after finishing his second term of Governor, that the Sheriff's boys began calling for his household effects to satisfy importunate creditors. It was the lecture platform that saved him, just as it later saved Alf" (Augsburg, 1925, p. 61). Robert Taylor turned to the lecture circuit, traveling throughout the country and giving prepared speeches amalgamating reminiscences, allegories, storytelling, and personal conjecture.

In 1891, Taylor's tour of his speech 'The Fiddle and the Bow' was reported to have an expected a "hundred lectures in Southern cities" ("From Stump," 1891). "The records kept by DeLong Rice, Bob Taylor's manager, show that $75,000 was taken in at the doors and more than a score of Confederate monuments were erected throughout the South" (Augsburg, 1925, p. 66). The United Daughters of the Confederacy was founded in Nashville, Tennessee, in 1894, so the fundraising for these statues predates their existence. Discussions about Confederate monuments started as early as 1866, and there seemed to be controversy even at this early stage.

General Philip Sheridan, on July 18, 1866, issued General Order No. 14 in New Orleans "prohibiting the erection, in this military division, of any monument commemorating the rebellion" ("An Order," 1866) as well as "dissolving all organizations for that purpose" ("Military Order,"

1866). Specifically, the order stated, "Notification is hereby given, for the information of all concerned, that no monument intended to commemorate the late rebellion will be permitted to be erected within limits of the military division of the Gulf" ("General Sheridan's," 1866). Sheridan was in charge of the 5th Military District encompassing Texas and Louisiana. The order seemed to be a hot-button issue, perhaps with the opposite of what was intended with groups, such as veterans from Texas' Hood's Brigade intentionally violating it ("A Confederate," 1866). Newspapers reported it was "not complied with in the country parishes, and only had an effect in a few cities" ("The Rebels," 1866). Confederate veterans may have also used other organizations for their cause. "A great many Confederates have agreed to join the Fire Companies. ... It is well known that the Firemen of New Orleans have, at all times, taken an active part in politics" ("The Rebels," 1866).

Robert Love Taylor, in all likelihood, was the first person who brought widespread attention to the idea of a Mammy monument. The genesis is a line in his lecture series that began in the fall of 1893. In August and September 1893, newspaper articles promoted his upcoming lecture, 'The Paradise of Fools.' He began delivering it in mid to late October 1893, starting in East Tennessee. Some of its earliest performances were in Johnson City on October 18 and Morristown on October 19, 1893. Within this speech, Taylor talks about his childhood in idealized memory. He recounts stories of his youth and then describes a story with his Mammy. He says, "The day will come when the South will build a monument to the good old Black mammy of the past for the lullabies she has sung" (Taylor, 1912, p. 54). He delivered this lecture regularly throughout the United States through at least December 1897 ("Brief Mention," 1897). His tribute to his Mammy was a highlight of his performance where apparently "With daring originality he sang the lullaby of the old 'mammy' nurse of Southern babyhood..." ("The Editors," 1894). Throughout the various newspaper accounts, it is heavily implied he gave this song with an affected vernacular to evoke the linguistic traits embodying the most traditional stereotypes commonplace when referencing slaves. These lectures matter in a broader political context because they were used as justification to extol Southern mammies while simultaneously restricting full participation within wider society. This duality helps engrain an almost caste-like system of citizenship that allows for depriving rights framed as protectionism. The mammy is idolized but constrained within an imagined space where she exists only as an agentless servant.

JAMES THOMAS "COTTON TOM" HEFLIN

James Thomas "Cotton Tom" Heflin is primarily remembered today as the Alabama legislator who created Mother's Day within the United States. Heflin was elected to various roles within government throughout his career, serving in Alabama state government, the U.S. House of Representatives, and the U.S. Senate. While serving in the House in 1913, Heflin introduced HR 103 on May 10, 1913, encouraging officials to wear white carnations to honor mothers. He introduced formal legislation a year later, designating the second Sunday in May as Mother's Day (*Historical Highlights*, n.d.). Heflin was a "pious Methodist who abstained from coffee, tea, alcohol, and tobacco, and allegedly felt that God guided his ever action" (Harper, 1968, p. 390). He was called 'Cotton Tom' "because of his repeated promises to raise the prices of Alabama's money crop" (Harper, 1968, p. 392).

James Thomas Heflin was a delegate at the Alabama Constitutional Convention in 1901. His presence at this convention was successful enough that he successfully ran for Alabama secretary of state the following year. Heflin gave a speech at the constitutional convention advocating for the disenfranchisement of Black Alabamans. He did not want to extend the right to vote. In his speeches in front of the convention, he refuses to allow for Black suffrage yet crafts a position where he believes in homage but not agency. In one breath, Heflin rejects Black franchise while simultaneously paying tribute to his mammy, proclaiming we should have statues for our mammies, given what they have done for the country. "Heflin said, 'I believe as truly as I believe that I am standing here that God Almighty intended the negro to the servant of the white man'" (Bond, 1939, p. 173). Heflin continues with, "I am not an enemy of the negro; I am a friend to him in his place. ... He was in his place as a slave, and happy and contented as such... as Governor Taylor says, I believe the time will come when the South will erect a monument to the old black mammy for the lullaby she has sung" (Bond, 1939, p. 173). By paraphrasing the section of Taylor's lecture almost verbatim, Heflin shows the power and sway of the 'Paradise of Fools' over Southern beliefs at this point in time.

Heflin believed Blacks were "not merely subordinate to the white race, but he was ordained by God to be the white man's servant" (Hackney, 1969, p. 204). Heflin strongly opposed equality in education, asserting "some day the clash will come and survival of the fittest, and I do not believe it is incumbent upon us to lift him up and education him on an equal footing that he may be armed and equipped when the combat comes" (Hackney, 1969, p. 205). These ideas are consistent with the views of eugenic beliefs in racial competition. Within these views, conflict is inevitable, especially with those considered at lower levels of human evolution (Weikart, 2004, p. 170). Perceived inferior groups will eventually lose but will agitate and be brutal. Hegemons go against their best interests by allowing them any concessions toward equality. The president of the Alabama Constitutional Convention was John B. Knox. In his opening remarks, he states, "it is, within the limits imposed by the Federal Constitution, to establish White supremacy in this State" ("Journal," 1901, p. 9). For Heflin, White supremacy meant restriction of suffrage and careful elimination of access to any power for racial minorities. During testimony at this convention, the report given by Richard Channing Jones from the Suffrage and Elections Committee stated the following referring to Black voting. "He would not know what to do with it if he had it. I would just as soon give a toddling child a razor in his hand expecting him not to hurt himself, as to expect the negro to use the ballot and not use it to his injury and to ours" ("Official Proceedings," 1901, p. 2880). In Alabama, by 1906, only 2 percent of the Black male population was registered to vote, and that ratio continued until the 1960s (Hackney, 1969, p. 206). "The convention did its job well: white voters declined, Negro voters practically ceased to exist" (Hackney, 1969, p. 208).

This event links race, statuary, and personal rights together. Heflin espoused a paternalistic love for his mammy but wanted to stop short of anything close to equality. Statues were acceptable to allow persons of color to see appropriate modeling, but the extension of voting rights was intolerable. In fact, in 1908, Heflin shot a Black man in the head on a streetcar who was drinking near a woman. Heflin, who was angered when the man would not refrain from drinking near the woman, forcibly removed him from the streetcar and shot him. He later justified his actions by saying "I have since learned that the Negro was a dangerous character with a bad court record" ("Cowardly Assault," 1908). "He was indicted but never convicted and continued to hold his seat in the U.S. House for another twenty-four years, bragging the shooting was the highlight of his career" (Kelley, 2010, p. 160). James Thomas Heflin believed in White superiority in every facet of his life.

THE USAGE OF MAMMY TO CRAFT ACCEPTABLE SOCIAL ROLES

Mammy statuary and Confederate memorials are utterly intertwined with each other within the worldview of modeling appropriate societal roles and power imbalance. Both reflect the need to convey and espouse expectations as well as values. Mammies, or broadly, faithful slave statues, demonstrate the appropriate place of persons of color within society. They are servants, caregivers, and pliant subordinates who exist to attend to the needs of their superiors. They lack any agency or interior lives. Statuaries honoring them allow for broader insinuations about what is and is not acceptable in society concerning persons of color. These statues provide literal, concrete models of the role of a Black person in American culture. Likewise, confederate memorials reframe the remembrance of the Civil War with the defeated side as noble defenders of their way of life. McElya (2007) argues that depictions of the faithful slave speak to "expressions of the value, honor and identity of whites. They had little if anything to do with the actual perceptions and attitudes of the enslaved" (p. 6). Furthermore, idealized notions of a Mammy also signal your family was sufficiently wealthy in the Antebellum period that you could afford the luxury of enslaved house servants.

Within the broader American society, there seemed to be a generalized interest in codifying the image of a Mammy by the early twentieth century. According to *The Macon Telegraph*, on September 20, 1910, a group called the Black Mammy Memorial Institute filed for incorporation. "The purpose of the school is to teach the present generation of the colored race the domestic science, and knowledge of the affairs of the home, that were possessed by the black mammy of antebellum days, in addition to the improvement of agriculture and economy in household affairs" ("Black Mammy," 1910). A paper on October 8, 1910 in Mississippi referred to this institute as a

> great benefit to a large class of young negros and of much value to the white people who have to depends on the colored race for house servants. … The young negroes of the present time being so imbued with the idea of personal freedom and equal rights may be disinclined to pay indirect

tribute to the memory of the 'black mammy,' who was the product of benevolent servitude. ("Good Cooks," 1910)

The last news article on this institute was in June 1912 when *The Macon Telegraph* reported on the upcoming dedication exercises on June 14 ("Gov. Brown," 1912). The school's construction was never completed, though they did begin teaching courses. "Few documents exist that discuss the school's demise, except records that mention how the land was returned several years later to the city of Athens to be used in other facilities" (Knight, 2007, p. 112). It is possible the organization's goals were more complex than simple training of persons in the skills of a mammy. It brought attention to black education and, more importantly, inequalities of Black education (Knight, 2007, p. 113) which may have been why it received support from their community. It appears this institute received support from Whites because it perhaps helped encourage their views of appropriate places and roles within society for persons of color. Persons of color supported it, perhaps not out of agreement, but because it brought attention to inequalities in segregated education environments.

The year 1910 was also notable for a proposed Mammy statue in Galveston, Texas. "It is planned to build a marble monument of appropriate design to cost $500,000, nearly half of which is already pledged" ("To Erect," 1910). On December 26, 1910 in Galveston, Arthur J. Baum, who, according to newspaper accounts, "inaugurated the movements a few months back to the 'black mammy,' committed suicide at a hotel" ("Arthur," 1910). This organization's president, composed of 'Old Black Mammy's White Folks,' was T. J. Groce, the president of the Galveston National Bank ("Will Erect," 1910). Groce died of a cerebral hemorrhage on August 2, 1911, and there were legal actions concerning his bank and mergers over the next year (*Oakleigh*, 2020). While somewhat unclear regarding specific details, the momentum for a Galveston monument stalled, but the idea remained. The *Austin American-Statesman* on January 21, 1912, reported what was now apparently called the "Old Black Mammy Monument Association" had started in Galveston, "The monument is to be erected in a Southern city, this city to be selected by a vote of the members of the association" ("A Monument," 1912) while making a pitch its placement in Austin. This monument does not appear to have been completed, though it does help spawn similar attempts.

There was an announcement in June 1915 about a different mammy monument that members of the 'Old Guard of Atlanta' "met at the University of Alabama Club recently and decided that this monument should be erected near Piedmond [Piedmont] Park, in Atlanta, in the near future, showing her as she appeared in the old days, just after slavery ceased" ("Monument to," 1915). The idea of erecting monuments to faithful Mammy slaves grew and spread throughout the South. As the country moved away from the Civil War, memorials became the way to provide historical memory. In 2022, the Southern Poverty Law Center found there are still 723 monuments, 741 roadways, 51 buildings, 38 parks, and 22 holidays honoring Confederates within the United States ("Whose Heritage," 2022). According to the map, most were erected between 1900 and 1920 (Ahmed, 2017).

Why Does Statuary Matter?

These statues are not about memorials but about cultivating memory. Moments within our lives are fleeting. Most of us cannot predict which events of our days will be cornerstone occasions or forgettable instances. Statues ensure their backers' perspectives retain their place within the culture. The majority of Southerners could not afford plantations of slaves. A nursemaid was a luxury afforded to only the most wealthy. Supporting Mammy statues functions as virtue and wealth signaling to peers within a community. It is also not too far of a leap to compare these sorts of statutes to the tactics of the NAACP in the 1950s, though it is on the other side of the coin. In the quest for dismantling segregation in education, the NAACP initially focused on higher education because they understood elementary school education would be a flashpoint, given many people have or have had young children. Collegiate education was less threatening to society and provided a basis to achieve cases to use as precedent to extend to all levels of education. Mammy statues utilize the same mindset but in a different direction. Mammy statues offer the image of a loving, non-threatening material figure. An editorial in 1923 supporting a statue refers to a mammy as "a character without a parallel. ... Certain abstract theories that somebody was 'fighting for her freedom' conveyed no meaning to her mind. The enemies of her 'white folks' were her enemies..." ("Honor," 1923). Much like targeting collegiate education, pushing for Mammy statues is a non-threatening way to instill values to society. The NAACP wanted to desegregate education for broader equality. Mammy statues sought to show the path persons of color were expected to follow for White acceptance. Eugenics is not simply about better breeding but also about understanding societal hierarchy. Mammy statues, memorials, and other remembrances make sure everyone remembers who was in service to whom while giving it a hazy veneer. Mammys are trusted with children but are also referred to in child-like terms. Continuing the quote above about enemies of her 'White folks,' the following line says, "so far as any notion of hostility could find lodging in her simple and loving nature" ("Honor," 1923). White society needs to entrench itself into the superior status while positioning Black memory in ways they prefer as well. Mammy statues, erected on a platform or base above the average citizen's height, elevate it above us all. It requires people to raise their heads to look at it, much like a person who listens to a speaker at a podium. A mammy statue teaches us through modeling the acceptable role of a Black person within American society. Compliant, friendly, slightly naïve, and unquestioningly faithful servants are the archetypes those creating these memorials value. It is the story they want to construct and pass off to subsequent generations as factual.

How Titles Signal Power

Honorifics in society tell us who and who not to afford respect. Etiquette developed as "a system that afformed the aristocracy as a group" (Arditi, 1998, p. 3). In modern society, children are frequently addressed as master and miss. We rarely use those terms toward adults. "All black men, on the other hand, were called by their first names or were referred to as 'Boy,' 'Uncle,' and 'Old Man'- regardless of their age" (Davis, n.d.). Likewise, "Black women were addressed as 'Auntie' or 'girl.' Under no circumstances would the title 'Miss' or 'Mrs.' be applied" (Davis, n.d.). These rules, while unwritten in many places, were considered acceptable norms. Reserving titles like "'Mr.' and 'Mrs.' for white men and women were the chief form of everyday social control in the segregated South" (Rittenhouse, 2007, p. 20). These terms were used to enforce hierarchy. Rev. Dr. Edward Wilkinson Lampton was forced to flee Greenville, Mississippi, in 1909 because of "threats resulted from one of his daughters who asked the white saleswomen and telephone operator to address her as Ms. Lampton" ("Founder's Day," 2022). In 1939, a Black servant named Eloise Blake "was charged $15... for calling another colored woman 'Mrs.' over the telephone of her white employer" (Myers, 1939, p. 23).

When she asked to speak to Mrs. Pauline Clay instead of just Pauline, the employer was so offended they "called an officer and had charges preferred against Mrs. Blake for 'disorderly conduct over the telephone'" (Myers, 1939, p. 23). The terminology offended the employer, so she contacted the police, who issued Eloise Blake a fine for using a term that should only apply to Whites. Persons of color had different titles. Terms like Aunt or Uncle were given to Black persons to ensure they understood their social place. These terms were somewhat more respectful (Rittenhouse, 2007, p. 21) and would often be applied to a favored person (McMillen, 1990, p. 23). White persons were Misters, Missus, or Sir and Ma'am. Black persons were called Uncle, Aunt, or even Mammy to make sure the societal hierarchy remained intact.

Furthermore, when a casual acquaintance or unknown White person calls a Black person Aunt or Uncle, they impose a cordiality. These terms also imply a familiarity even when none exists. Rittenhouse (2007) points out, "Internalizing racial etiquette allowed many whites to convince themselves that theirs was an honorable society and that blacks did believe in national racial hierarchy, despite overwhelming evidence of black resistance" (p. 24). It is why brands like 'Aunt Jemima,' or 'Uncle Bens' began to be immersed in controversy, leading to name alterations and changes in 2021. The perpetuation of imagery of the loyal Black servant whose entire existence centers around domestic pride flattens individuals into smiling caricatures. They no longer exist as people but as avatars for roles assigned to them to model idealized behavior.

Mammy Memorial at the National Level

Confederate Memorial at Arlington National Cemetery

The most comprehensive and successful push for a Mammy monument was at the national level. The United Daughters of the Confederacy, an organization dedicated to the memory of the Southern cause, had been an active participant in helping erect memorials throughout the South in the early twentieth century. The group was founded in 1894, though smaller regional groups existed before that time. The primary focus for this organization involved raising money to support the memory of their view of the Civil War and raising funds for memorials. The largest and most notable memorial they ever achieved was the Confederate Memorial at Arlington National Cemetery. Standing 32.5 feet tall (Johnson,

2000, p. 22), it has a relief in the round depicting various scenes of soldiers marching to war. The Civil War in these representations creates a reminiscence of the noble fight where men embraced the lost cause in honor of their home. The war's outcome takes a secondary seat in favor of the defense of Southern culture and nostalgic memory. "The memorial was dedicated by President Woodrow Wilson on June 4, 1914, the 106th anniversary of the birth of Confederate President Jefferson Davis" (Johnson, 2000, p. 22). This monument frames Black support for the Southern cause in a positive light. The chairman of the Arlington Confederate Monument Association executive committee, Hillary A. Herbert, wrote a long booklet entitled *History of the Arlington Confederate Monument* to help remember it in the most accurate way possible. He was in charge and best positioned to explain the events leading to its creation. Therefore, his descriptions of the reliefs in this account must be taken at their face value as their intentional meaning. Herbert's written account and documentation are the closest to their accurate intention. While the entire monument is interesting, two sections of the relief are notable in the context of faithful slave memorials. First, there is a Black man in the background in one section. According to Herbert, he "is a faithful negro body-servant following his young master, Mr. Thomas Nelson Page's realistic 'Marse Chan' over again" (Herbert, 1914, p. 77). A body servant refers to a person who was the personal servant of a soldier. "These men performed a wide range of roles for their owners, including cooking, cleaning, foraging and sending messages to families back home" (Levin, 2019). Body servants could range from very young to quite elderly. They were also considered highly loyal to their family, but they were also slaves with no choice as to whether to accompany their owners to war.

The reference to Marse Chan refers to Page's 1887 book, *In Ole Virginia or Marse Chan and Other Stories*. Like *Plunkitt of Tammany Hall*, Page's book switches into a dialect style to capture the vernacular and speaking style of its subjects. Marse Chan is set in 1872, and the main character, Sam, regales a White stranger with stories about his young master Tom Channing, or 'Marse Chan.' When his owner goes off to war, Sam joins him. The book is an antebellum idyllic tale with the main character saying, "Dem wuz good ole times, marster – de bes' Sam uver see!" (Page, 1888, p. 13). His owner dies in the war, and from the tone and scope of the tale, Channing's remaining lands are a shadow of their former self, with strong insinuations that the world before the war was far preferable. The relief on the Arlington memorial shows a faithful servant marching to his potential death as support staff for his owner. The body servant is not a soldier but a caregiver to facilitate their owner's wants and needs, even during war. The servant lacks agency because they exist to be useful and thus are depicted as their master sees them, regardless of reality.

The second section of the relief involves "an officer, kissing his child in the arms of an old negro 'mammy,' Another child holds on to the skirts of the 'mammy' and is crying, perhaps without knowing why" (Herbert, 1914, p. 77). The mammy, who does not appear elderly, looks at the man with concern while the child reaches in for what looks to be a last kiss from a father already in a military formation. The emotion in this scene draws itself from the Mammy's face and the body language of the children. Over the years, this section has been the subject of lasting criticism. Faithful slaves serve their masters without question and with utter devotion. She is watching her owner leave for a battle while giving a last desperate goodbye to his small children. It is telling all the emotion in this section relies upon the children and their mammy servant. The children's mother is not depicted, suggesting she was not considered relevant enough to be included in this part of the memorial. Both faithful slaves lack agency and demonstrate unquestioning fidelity to their owners.

In September 2022, an independent commission exploring Confederate commemoration recommended the removal of the memorial from Arlington as part of the final report (Baldor, 2022). My December 2022 visit found it was no longer part of the Arlington standard tour for the cemetery. The memorial was somewhat isolated in a section removed from much of the tour, though busses drove near it between stops. The memorial was about a 15-minute walk from the closest standardized tour stop location. The bus tour guides indicated they were allowed to answer questions when asked, but content about it was no longer part of their monologues to groups.

When removing the monument began moving forward, some protest groups filed legal action with a restraining order that temporarily stopped the process (Barakat, 2023). The filing to prevent removal focused upon the potential desecration of graves as justification for leaving it in place ("Judge Allows," 2023). The presiding judge allowed for the removal in December 2023 noting there was no evidence of any potential desecration and considerable care was being taken to protect the surrounding graves (Alfonseca, 2023). As of early 2024, it had been removed from the location with plans to relocate it to the grounds of the New Market

Battlefield State Historical Park in the Shenandoah Valley ("Confederate Memorial," 2023).

National Mammy Statue

The success of the memorial monument in Arlington likely helped encourage the United Daughters of the Confederacy to continue their objective to create more monuments and memorials that recast the Civil War as a noble and just cause for the South. While other Mammy memorials had been at the local level, this one would be a national memorial enshrining the Mammy as part of American memory. The push for this Mammy statue occurred in 1923 in the U. S. Congress at the urging of Jefferson Davis Chapter 1650 of the United Daughters of the Confederacy. McElya (2007) argues, "The mammy figure cemented the Daughters' elite status within the public realm as southern ladies and confirmed their authority over black labor and behavior" (p. 145). On December 8. 1922, Senator John Sharp Williams introduced the bill (S 4119) "authorizing the erection in the city of Washington of a monument to the memory of the faithful colored mammies of the South during the war between the States" (Williams, 1922, p. 209). Williams was the ranking member of the Senate Committee of the Library and left at the end of this session. Senator Williams spent about 30 years in government, from the 1890s through the 1920s. His views on White supremacy are salient in helping understand his later support for a memorial of this type. As a United States House of Representatives member, he engaged in a December 20, 1898, debate over extending voting and other rights to the indigenous populations in the Philippines and other Pacific regions. Representative Williams's words are essential because they help frame the same person who, about 25 years later, wants to honor mammys.

> Individual accomplishment is skin deep, Mr. Chairman: hereditary traits, tendencies, and capabilities are inbred to the marrow of our bones. Why, Mr. Chairman, you could shipwreck 10,000 illiterate white Americans or Englishmen or Scotchmen, of who not one knew a letter in a book, on a desert island, and in three weeks they would have a fairly good government ... You could shipwreck and equal number of American Indians, every man of whom is a graduate of Hampden-Sidney or Carlisle, or 10,000 negroes, every one of whom was a graduate of Harvard University, and in less than three years, they would have retrograded governmentally to the old tribal

relations, half the men would have been killed and the other half would have two wives a piece. (Williams, 1898, p. 342)

Williams also proudly defended Mississippi's capacity to disfranchise non-Whites with literacy tests. He declared they were able to "secure for the electorate a majority safe for white supremacy and civilization" (Williams, 1898, p. 342). Williams believed in White superiority and the importance of others understanding their place in society. His support of a mammy statue aligns with his long-standing beliefs about American culture. The legislation was referred to the House Committee on the Library. According to a news piece, the United Daughters of the Confederacy would erect the monument ("Favors," 1923). The Senate bill left the committee on February 28, 1923, waiting for the House of Representatives to move forward. On January 5, 1923, Charles Stedman introduced the House legislation (HR 13672) for the Mammy statue. Representative Stedman, a Democrat representing North Carolina's 5th district, was eventually the last veteran of the Civil War from either side serving in Congress. The *Congressional Record* states "a bill (HR 13672) authorizing the erection in the city of Washington a monument in the memory of the faithful colored mammies of the South" (Stedman, 1923, p. 1347) without any commentary. News articles of the day tell a different story. One article recounts the entire "membership, Republicans and Democrats, cheered Mr. Stedman for several minutes when he began, and after he had praised the negro mammy of ante-bellum days, he was given another round of applause" ("Gray Vet," 1923). The applause is likely because Stedman was hinting at retiring at the end of this session, though he ultimately stayed until 1930. Another similar news piece said the Stedman "painted the negro mammy's fidelity as without parallel in history and the erection of the monument would mark one of the few times when a people had so honored one of another race living among them" ("House Cheers," 1923).

The *Evening Star*, a Washington, D.C. newspaper, reported on organized opposition in their community. The Northeast Boundary Citizens' Association called the proposal "propaganda to divert attention from the wrongs done colored women during the civil war and the reconstruction period that followed" ("Memorial to," 1923). Mary Church Terrell, an African-American activist and among the first Black women to earn a college degree, wrote a letter to the editor of the *Evening Star* as the

Honorary President of the National Association of Colored Women. She pointed out that a mammy

> was often faithful in the service of her mistress' children, while her own heart bled over her own little babies who were thus deprived of their mother's ministrations and tender care which the white children received. ... the anguish of one black mammy whose children were snatched away from her embrace and sold away from her forever outweighed in the balance all the kindness bestowed upon the slave women fortunate enough to receive it in the 250 years. ("The Black Mammy," 1923)

There appeared to be an organized and vocal opposition to the statue. Ultimately, the legislation died in the House of Representatives without any action. "Three months after the introduction of the monument bill in the Senate, Congress adjourned without having taken any further action" (Horwitz, 2013). However, the bill's timing has interesting aspects, suggesting that many in Congress were preparing to eliminate it, albeit less aggressively. During this period, Congress had a House Committee on the Library, a Senate Committee on the Library, and a Joint Committee on the Library. The Senate committee was chaired by Frank B. Brandegee (R-CT), and John Sharp Williams (D-MS) was the ranking member. The House committee was chaired by Norman J. Gould (R-NY), and Frank Park (D-GA) was the ranking member. The 67th Congress adjourned on March 3, 1923. The Senate bill (S. 4119) was introduced on December 8, 1922. The House of Representatives version (HR 13672) was introduced on January 5, 1923.

The committee's ranking member, Senator Williams, introduced it in the Senate. The House version was introduced by Charles Stedman, who was not on the House or Joint Committee on the Library at this time. The bill passed the Senate and was referred to the House's Committee on the Library on Wednesday, February 28, 1923. Congress was adjourned sine die on Saturday, March 3, 1923. All bills not signed into law by the end of the session must start the entire process again when the 68th Congress convenes. Norman Gould was the Republican representative for Seneca County, New York, when that area was synonymous with expanding suffrage rights for women. House Committee Chair Gould announced he had decided not to seek reelection on June 9, 1922 ("Gould," 1922). Newspaper accounts indicated Gould was not often in Washington and was frequently absent during the 67th Congress (Kirchhofer, 1922).

More briefly stated, the Senate bill was referred to a committee in the House of Representatives with two days left on the calendar. Additionally, it was sent to a committee with a retiring and frequently absent chairman. His absence would make scheduling a vote difficult in the most optimal situation. Even in the best circumstances, these timing constraints would be challenging for any bill to be reconciled and sent for a final vote in Congress. It would then need to head to the president for a signature or veto. While not definitive, the timing could have circumvented the passage without direct opposition.

On December 31, 1923, a news article reported the location which had been selected. "The bill granting the site in Washington, D.C. on Massachusetts Ave, near Sheridan Circle was proposed in the Senate by John Sharp Williams" ("Plan Statue," 1923). This news piece, well after the close of the 67th Congress, suggests that the United Daughters of the Confederacy were still hopeful that the bill would find its way to be reintroduced in the next session, and they were proceeding optimistically. Representative Stedman reintroduced the bill to the House (HR 6253) on January 26, 1924, but it appears to have not generated any substantial interest (Stedman, 1924, p. 1516). A short news piece in April 1924 declared the bill allowing the Daughters of the Confederacy "to erect a Black Mammy statue was killed for good and all by a committee in the House recently" ("No Mammy," 1924).

Eventually, in 2002, another statue was put in this location. A statue of Thomas Garrigue Masaryk was placed in a triangular area at the intersection of Q Street NW, 22nd Street NW, and Massachusetts Avenue. Masaryk was the first president of Czechoslovakia, a supporter of his nation's independence, and supported his nation embracing democracy.

OTHER MEMORIALS AND MEMORY

While not a mammy, in 1927, a monument in Natchitoches, Louisiana, was created with a plaque reading "dedicated to the arduous and faithful services of the good darkies of Louisiana" (Daugherty, 2019, p. 631). This statue is known as Good Darky and Uncle Jack. The statue is of an older Black man with hunched shoulders, tipping his hat and lowering his head to persons in front of him. The implication of the statue is overt. A Black man's place is to show appropriate abeyance to his superiors. It echoes as a theme throughout faithful slave statuary. While often framed as a tribute, it is a lesson of proper expectation of accepted behavior. The statue was funded by Jackson Lee (J. L.) Bryan, a Natchitoches banker and cotton planter. When asked about the statue, Bryan said, "I found it strange that no one had encouraged the faithful old souls even by saying as much as 'Well done, thou good and faithful servant,' and accordingly I decided to say it myself this way" ("Southern Town," 1927). Another newspaper account in this period described this statue as "he stands, hat in hand, the eager faithful figure, ready to help in any way Ole Marse or Ole Miss may wish- a living reminder to the present generation of the affectionate bond between old slaves and their owners" ("Statue to," 1928). In April 1934, an article published in several Louisiana newspapers also discussed the statue. This piece was created by the Louisiana Tourist Bureau and referred to this statue as "standing in perpetual protest against certain legends and traditions which connect some of the surrounding sections with the cruelties depicted in 'Uncle Tom's Cabin'" (Goldstein, 1934). The Harriet Beecher Stowe novel, written in 1852, has portions set in Louisiana, where the state is negatively depicted. The newspaper accounts link this statue with reframing Stowe's portrayal into a more positive one. Bryan's Louisiana was a location where Blacks were friendly, loyal, and obedient. Their owners pay tribute to that gracious servitude with this statue. This statue has been controversial since even before its creation and stood for forty-one years before it was removed and a few years later "relocated and recontextualized in a less traveled, less public institutional site at the Rural Life Museum of Louisiana State University in Baton Rouge" (Daugherty, 2019, p. 631).

Passive, friendly, obedient servants who know their place and role in society do not challenge hierarchies. Monuments to them signal who is valued and what sort of attitudes are accepted. White Americans who advocate for faithful slave memorials usurp the agency and stories of the actual servants in favor of their preferred narratives. It seems many confuse passive resistance with guileless naivety. Persons without power in many systems employ what is often referred to as weapons of the weak as an essential survival tactic. Scott (1985) refers to open defiance toward American slavery as foolhardy (p. 33).

> The history of resistance to slavery in the antebellum U.S. South is largely a history of foot dragging, false compliance, flight, feigned ignorance,

sabotage, theft, and, and not least, cultural resistance. ... The slaves themselves appear to have realized that in most circumstances their resistance could succeed only to the extent that it hid behind the mask of public compliance. (Scott, 1985, p. 34)

In other words, the supposed faithful slave was likely, in many cases, a necessary survival tactic existing as a docile, compliant living mannequin.

The National Manassas Battlefield in Manassas, Virginia shows clear distinctions in memorial and memory. The memorial at Henry Hill is one of the very first monuments created for soldiers in the Civil War. National Parks Service refers to it as the 'Patriots Monument.' It is a Union monument to remember those who died at Bull Run in 1861. It was completed in June 1865. The memorial was created by soldiers "in one of their final acts before discharge" ("Patriots Monument," 2022). It is an important monument because it reflects the memory of soldiers who chose to remember their fallen comrades. The descendants of veterans did not create this memorial. Instead, it was crafted by the living for their fellow soldiers who died. It is a simple memorial standing 27 feet high, made of sandstone ("Dedication," n.d.). It is in the shape of an obelisk with artillery shells at specific points surrounding it. The monument is simple and direct and would likely be considered an appropriate stone for a cemetery or graveyard. This monument functions as a memorial created by soldiers, and does not want to reframe grief into a tool for memory. On the same battlefield area near the obelisk is the statue commemorating Stonewall Jackson's Confederate victory. The idea for this statue started in 1936 and was unveiled in 1940 ("Stonewall" 2023). This 20-foot-tall statue looks distinctly different from the obelisk. Jackson sits in a heroic pose atop his horse with the phrase 'There stands Jackson like a stone wall' carved into the base.

Jackson looks more like Superman than a soldier, without an ounce of fat on his overly muscular frame. His chest and arm muscles strain against his uniform, barely containing them. His cape rests like a superhero, framing his back. His horse stands proud as well. The extremely overly muscular horse looks like it powerlifts as a recreational hobby. The towering image of Jackson sends a strong message of heroism with the expectation of idolization. Those from a later time placed this sculpture after the veterans had mainly passed away, and it helped serve as a framing of the Confederate general. He exists as a superman, strong and superior to the common man. This statue is not just about remembering the Battle of Manassas but remembering it in a particular way.

Memorials are not all about generals or military campaigns. Frank E. Davidson, of Sumter County, Alabama, built a memorial to his slaves, which garnered attention in 1912. Dr. Davidson, a dentist and war veteran, placed on his plantation near Belmont a marble monument to the "faithfulness of his former servants, whom he never allowed to be whipped or abused, and stated they refused to leave him after the war, but lived and died on his plantation in his service" ("Monument to Ex-Slaves," 1912). Articles espouse Davidson's kindness (Davidson, 1924, p. 4), but none recount the names of the persons he remembered. While heralded for creating a monument unlike any other, it also focuses upon his paternal guidance that endeared his nameless slaves to him. Articles mention he listed their first names, but only in passing. These memorials focus attention on the idolized memory. Dr. Davidson's slaves are remembered but only stand out because of their faithful and loyal service to him. Their actions are only meaningful in reference to their protection of their master.

The Intersection of Mammy Statues and Immigration Legislation

These statues, especially the national push for the mammy statue, remain important and salient in the context of other issues. The ideas of superiority, modeling behavior, and acceptability do not fade away with the death of a bill. The debate over Mammy statues largely ended when the bill failed to leave the House of Representatives in the 67th session of Congress. About fourteen months later, one of the most significant immigration bills in the United States was introduced on May 26, 1924. The Immigration Act of 1924, also known as the Johnson-Reed Act, puts severe limitations upon immigration with stark favoritism toward Western European nations. Often, we think of legislation in isolation, away from more significant cultural ramifications. The reality, however, is these issues are linked, with overlapping groups that often look like Venn diagrams. There was a large eugenics display in the halls of Congress for months before the passage of the Immigration Restriction Bill in 1924 (Chase, 1977, p. 291; Hasian, 1996, p. 43). Harry H. Laughlin testified in front of the House of Representatives's Committee on Immigration and Naturalization in 1920 about racial concerns over immigration. At the immigration committee meeting on April 17, 1920, Laughlin said, "Whenever two races come in contact, it is found that the women of the lower race are not, as a rule, adverse to intercourse with men of the higher. And that has been true throughout history. It is true now" (Laughlin, 1920, p. 15). He was almost certainly using scare tactics in pursuit of his larger immigration aims within society, but all these ideas were within their world at the same time. They did not exist within a vacuum isolated from each other. Given the timing of these two major issues dealing with racial superiority, this eugenics display was likely to have been displayed shortly after or during the entire debate of a Mammy statue in Washington, D.C. According to testimony in Congress, Laughlin displayed figures and charts in the committee room for the House Committee on Immigration and Naturalization from December 13, 1921, to March 10, 1922 (Laughlin, 1922, p. 759).

This display in Congress came from portions of the eugenics exhibits at the Second International Congress on Eugenics. It was at the American Museum of National History in New York City from September to October 1921. "Many displays were returned to exhibitors, but those that 'pertained directly to immigration were installed on the walls of the [U.S. Congress's Committee on Immigration] in Washington for use of the Committee in analyzing certain historical and new data in reference to immigration'" (Rydell, 1993, p. 48). "The Eugenics Research Association displayed a chart beneath the Rotunda of the Capitol in Washington showing the costs to taxpayers supporting those Laughlin had described as 'social inadequates'" (Wright, 2008, p. 86). Laughlin was heavily involved with this research association and was, at one point, its president ("Eugenics Research," 1928).

Conclusion

Statues and statuary provide us with windows into our past. Most context and nuance within statues get lost over time. Every generation reads into a memorial, gleaning from the past through their lens of the present. As we change, so does our interpretation. Mammy statues and other faithful slave memorials function as a way for Whites to enshrine opinions toward appropriate behaviors of racial minorities within American life. Whites often referred to the 1923 Mammy statue as a racial peace statue. Peace, in this context, would occur if racial minorities passively and meekly accepted the role ascribed to them by Whites. Racial peace was a moniker put there by the majority to point at dissenters as the disruptive forces instead of themselves. While it is unlikely America would not again attempt to put up a literal mammy statue, ideas of White dominance still pervades culture. Majorities see their power as status quo, often dismissing any attempts to supplant or challenge it as immoral or degenerate. Mammy statuary engages viewers with the values of the past and forces those attitudes upon the observer to remain and not evolve past them. John Sharp Williams and J. Thomas Heflin proudly disenfranchised Blacks to retain White supremacy. Both also supported mammy monuments using the language of fond remembrance for a world only the wealthy few likely experienced. Mammy statues make sure poor Whites feel superior to Blacks while also making sure racial minorities understand the only place they will be accepted within a society.

Statuary allows for the modeling of norms and behavior. By constructing a narrative where mammys are faithful, loyal mother figures who embody a social ideal for a race, they also create a place for them to exist within a society. Black women are two dimensional, safe, loving figures who White people should see as maternal surrogates. Statues accentuating child-rearing or caregiving do not lend themselves to emulation in any other way within the greater world. It is reasonable to assume women who are members of the organizations like the United Daughters of the Confederacy, which were instrumental in pushing for these statues, wanted a safe description of the enslaved Black woman from both the past with an eye toward the present. Mammy statues make Black women safer as a construct within space. Organizations like the Black Mammy Memorial Institute lend credence to a subservient role as the only appropriate place within modern American life. White women were supportive of its aims and relentlessly fundraised for statuary to help entrench their hegemony within the accepted American family. Mammys are not exotic but loving mother figures. While not precisely the same, it is probably safe to say most women do not fantasize about dating Santa Claus. His paternal, grandfatherly role within a culture allows for the acknowledgment of him being male, but he exists fundamentally as an other within our lives. We want toys, comfort, and love from Santa, not a Tinder profile. Conjuring that image likely made several grin and others shudder. Consequently, mammy statuary honors women in a way but also works to ensure a line is drawn within American life. The appropriate role is modeled in permanence and erected for all to see. The overarching goals of racial purity within the era of eugenics extend into this realm and remain for all to see across time.

References

A Confederate Organization. (1866, October 4). *The Intelligencer*, p. 1.
A Monument to Sentiment. (1912, January 21). *Austin American-Statesman*, p. 5.
Ahmed, S. (2017, August 16). There are Certain Moments in US History When Confederate Monuments Go Up. *CNN*. https://www.cnn.com/2017/08/16/us/confederate-monuments-backlash-chart-trnd/index.html
Alfonseca, K. (2023, December 20). Judge Allows Removal of Confederate Statue at Arlington National Cemetery Amid Protests. *ABC News*. https://abcnews.go.com/US/judge-allows-removal-confederate-statue-arlington-national-cemetery/story?id=105773275#:~:text=Two%20of%20the%2032%20life,war%2C%22%20the%20cemetery%20states
An Order from Sheridan Against Confederate Monuments, & c. (1866, July 27). *The Abingdon Virginian*, p. 3.
Arditi, J. (1998) *A Genealogy of Manners: Transformations of Social Relations in France and England from the Fourteenth to the Eighteenth Century*. University of Chicago Press.
Arthur J. Baum A Suicide. (1910, December 27). *The Baltimore Sun*, p. 1.
Augsburg, P. D. (1925). *Bob and Alf Taylor: Their Lives and Lectures*. Morristown Book Company, Inc.
Baldor, L. C. (2022, September 12). Panel Advises Removal of Confederate Statue at Arlington. *Associated Press*. https://apnews.com/article/navy-army-congress-ty-seidule-government-and-politics-94fca53b29f7670d82f463c76fd1e39c
Barakat, M. (2023, December 18). Judge Issues Order Keeping Confederate Memorial at Arlington for Now. *Associated Press*. https://apnews.com/article/confederate-memorial-arlington-cemetery-restraining-order-65a00f0e3b49b22547059ee021ec3e82
Black Mammy Memorial is Seeking a Charter. (1910, September 21). *The Macon Telegraph*, p. 8.
Bond, H. M. (1939). *Negro Education in Alabama: A Study in Cotton and Steel*. The Associated Publishers, Inc.
Brief Mention. (1897, November 26). *The Commercial Appeal*, Memphis, Tennessee, p. 6.
Chase, A. (1977). *The Legacy of Malthus: The Social Costs of the New Scientific Racism*. Random House.
Confederate Memorial to Be Removed from Arlington National Cemetery. (2023, December 16). *Voice of America*. https://www.voanews.com/a/confederate-memorial-to-be-removed-from-arlington-national-cemetery-/7401330.html
Cowardly Assault. (1908, April 4). *The Washington Bee*, p. 1.

Daugherty, E. (2019). The Rise and Fall of a Racist Monument: The Good Darky, National Geographic Magazine and Civil Rights Activism. *Nineteenth Century Contexts*, *41*(4), 631–649.

Davidson, F. E. (1924, November 9). A Remarkable Plantation. *The Montgomery Advertiser*, p. 4.

Davis, R. L. F. (n.d.). Racial Etiquette: The Racial Customs and Rules of Racial Behavior in Jim Crow America. https://files.nc.gov/dncr-moh/jim%20crow%20etiquette.pdf

Dedication of the Battle Monument. (n.d.). *Encyclopedia Virginia*. https://encyclopediavirginia.org/809hpr-0a0bf32d3aba9ce/

Eugenics Research Association 16th Annual Meeting. (1928). *American Philosophical Society*. http://www.eugenicsarchive.org/html/eugenics/static/images/252.html

Favors Monument to Faithful Negro Mammies. (1923, January 31). *The Chattanooga News*, p. 12.

Founder's Day Ceremony for the Rev. Lampton. (2022, February 12). *The Delta Democrat-Times*, p. A9.

From Stump to Stage. (1891, November 1). *The Comet*, p. 5.

General Sheridan's Monumental Order-Alleged "Secret Rebel Societies." (1866, July 28). *The Daily Standard*, p. 2.

Goldstein, A. H. (1934, April 13). Know Louisiana. *Tensas Gazette*, p. 1.

Good Cooks Needed. (1910, October 8). *Jackson Daily News*, p. 4.

Gould Not to Run Again for House. (1922, June 10). *The New York Times*, p. 2.

Gov. Brown Speak Black Mammy Memorial. (1912, June 7). *The Macon Telegraph*, p. 13.

Gray Vet Pleads for 'Black Mammy' Statue. (1923, January 10). *The Tennessean*, p. 1.

Hackney, S. (1969). *Populism to Progressivism in Alabama*. Princeton University Press.

Harper, G. T. (1968). "Cotton Tom" Heflin and the Election of 1930. *The Historian*, *30*(3), 389–411.

Hasian, M. A., Jr. (1996). *The Rhetoric of Eugenics in Anglo-American Thought*. University of Georgia Press.

Herbert, H. A. (1914). *History of the Arlington Confederate Monument*. United Daughters of the Confederacy. https://www.battlefields.org/sites/default/files/atoms/files/History%20of%20the%20Arlington%20Confederate%20Monument.pdf

Historical Highlights: The First National Celebration of Mother's Day. (n.d.). The House of Representatives. Retrieved April 13, 2024. https://history.house.gov/HistoricalHighlight/Detail/35444

Honor to the Negro "Mammy." (1923, January 12). *The Macon News*, p. 6.

Horwitz, T. (2013, May 31). The Mammy Washington Almost Had. *The Atlantic.* https://www.theatlantic.com/national/archive/2013/05/the-mammy-washington-almost-had/276431/

House Cheers Talk for a Monument to the Negro "Mammy." (1923, January 10). *The Tampa Tribune*, p. 1.

Johnson, C. Arlington's Forgotten Monument. (2000, October). *Civil War Times Illustrated, 39*(5), 18–22.

Journal of the Alabama Constitutional Convention of 1901. (1901). *Alabama Department of Archives & History.* https://digital.archives.alabama.gov/digital/collection/constitutions/id/116/

Judge Allows the Removal of a Confederate Memorial at Arlington Cemetery. (2023, December 20). *National Public Radio.* https://www.npr.org/2023/12/20/1220573980/confederate-memorial-arlington-cemetery-removal

Kelley, B. M. (2010). *Right to Ride Streetcar Boycotts and African American Citizenship in the Era of Plessy v. Ferguson.* University of North Carolina Press.

Kirchhofer, A. H. (1922, October 6). Odds and Ends at the Capitol. *The Buffalo News*, p. 26.

Knight, M. D. (2007). *Seeking Education for Liberation: The Development of Black Schools in Athens, Georgia from Emancipation through Desegregation* [Doctoral Dissertation, University of Georgia]. https://getd.libs.uga.edu/pdfs/knight_monica_d_200708_phd.pdf

Laughlin, H. H. (1920, April 16–17). Biological Aspects of Immigration. Remarks in hearings before the House Committee on Immigration and Naturalization. Sixty-Sixth Congress, Second Session.

Laughlin, H. H. (1922, November 21). Analysis of America's Modern Melting Pot. Remarks in hearings before the House Committee on Immigration and Naturalization. Sixty-Seventh Congress, Third session.

Levin, K. M. (2019, July 2) The Diaries Left Behind by Confederate Soldiers Reveal the True Role of Enslaved Labor at Gettysburg. *Smithsonian Magazine.* https://www.smithsonianmag.com/history/diaries-left-behind-confederate-soldiers-reveals-role-enslaved-labor-gettysburg-180972538/

McElya, M. (2007). *Clinging to Mammy: The Faithful Slave in Twentieth-Century America.* Harvard University Press.

McMillen, N. (1990). *Dark Journey: Black Mississippians in the Age of Jim Crow.* University of Illinois Press.

Memorial to Colored 'Mammies' is Opposed. (1923, February 3). *Evening Star*, p. 9.

Military Order. (1866, July 26). *Daily Republican*, p. 3.

Monument to "Mammy." (1915, June 4). *Fort Worth Star-Telegram*, p. 2.

Monument to Ex-Slaves. (1912, June 26). *Our Southern Home*, p. 4.

Myers, I. M. A. (1939, August 4). Calls Friend 'Mrs.' Over Prone; Is Fined $15. *The Call*, p. 23.

No Mammy Statue. (1924, April 25). *The Monitor*, p. 1.
Oakleigh: Lost Southern Elegance 3112 Avenue O. (2020). *Galveston Monthly Magazine*. https://www.galvestonmonthly.com/homes/oakleigh.html
Official Proceedings of the Alabama Constitutional Convention 1901, vol. 3. (1901). *Alabama Department of Archives & History*. https://digital.archives.alabama.gov/digital/collection/constitutions/id/122/
Page, T. N. (1888). *In Ole Virginia or Marse Chan and Other Stories*. Charles Scribner's Sons.
Patriots Monument: Manassas National Battlefield Park. (2022, November 26). *National Park Service*. https://www.nps.gov/places/000/bull-run-monument.htm
Plan Statue to 'Black Mammy.' (1923, December 31). *Marysville Journal-Tribune*, p. 1.
Riordon, W. L. (1995). *Plunkett of Tammany Hall: A Series of Very Plain Talks on Very Practical Politics*. Signet Classic.
Rittenhouse, J. (2007). The Etiquette of Race Relations in the Jim Crow South. In T. Owney (Ed.), *Manners and Southern History* (pp. 20–44). University Press of Mississippi.
Rydell, R. W. (1993). *World of Fairs: The Century of Progress Expositions*. The University of Chicago Press.
Scott, J. C. (1985). *Weapons of the Weak: Everyday Forms of Peasant Resistance*. Yale University Press.
Southern Town Builds a Statue to Old Negroes. (1927, September 5). *The World-News*, p. 19.
Statue to a Darky. (1928, December 27). *The Natchitoches Enterprise*, p. 1.
Stedman, C. M. (1924, January 26). *House of Representatives Congressional Record*. Sixty-Eighth Congress, First Session (Vol. 65, part 2).
Stedman, C. M. (1923, January 5). *House of Representatives Congressional Record*. Sixty-Seventh Congress, Fourth Session (Vol. 64, part 2).
Stonewall Jackson Monument: Manassas National Battlefield Park. (2023, February 1). *National Park Service*. https://www.nps.gov/places/000/stonewall-jackson-monument.htm
Taylor, R. L. (1912). *Lectures and Best Literary Productions of Bob Taylor*. The Bob Taylor Publishing Co.
The Black Mammy Monument. (1923, February 10). *Evening Star*, p. 6.
The Editors. (1894, May 9). *Daily Arkansas Gazette*, p. 2.
The Rebels in Arms. (1866, September 11). *The Portland Daily Press*, p. 2.
To Erect $500,000 Mammy Statue. (1910, April 26). *Quad-City Times*, p. 1.
Weikart, R. (2004). *From Darwin to Hitler: Evolutionary Ethics, Eugenics, and Racism in Germany*. Palgrave Macmillan.

Whose Heritage? Public Symbols of the Confederacy, 3rd edition. (2022). *Southern Poverty Law Center.* https://www.splcenter.org/sites/default/files/whose-heritage-report-third-edition.pdf

Will Erect Monument to "Old Black Mammy." (1910, June 23). *The Florala News*, p. 1.

Williams, Rep. J. S. (1898, December 20). "Agricultural Appropriations Bill," Remarks in the House Congressional Record (Vol. 21, part 1). https://www.congress.gov/bound-congressional-record/1898/12/20/house-section

Williams, Sen. J. S. (1922, December 8). *Remarks in Senate Congressional Record* (Vol. 64, part 1, p. 209). https://www.congress.gov/bound-congressional-record/1922/12/08/senate-section

Wright, R. O. (2008). *Chronology of Immigration in the United States.* McFarland & Co.

CHAPTER 3

Immigration Laws and Eugenics

Abstract The United States has been shaped by immigration. This chapter explores the misconceptions and impact of early immigration leading up to the 1924 Immigration Act. Many poor English arrived as transported felons. They lacked rights and eventually, as time passed, reinvented themselves as simply Americans. The late nineteenth century saw the rise of very racially restrictive immigration laws. These were shaped by eugenics in an attempt to craft an idealized national identity. The chapter discusses the forces, ideas, and importance of the 1924 Immigration Act. The chapter looks at some congressional testimony about immigration from prominent eugenicists and how their perspectives impacted the legislation.

Keywords Transported felons · Immigration laws · Restrictive immigration · Non-hyphenated Americans · Laughlin

The United States is a nation conceived through immigration. Our entire character has been forged through the development of a country where none existed beforehand. Whom we have allowed in at different points shaped our country today. However, the reality of our origins is often at odds with our narrative. By better understanding our decisions and choices at different points, we can see how our past still shapes our future. Immigration into the United States has been a contentious topic long before its founding. The complex identity of American colonists has been washed clean via our passion play of Revolution. Our notable historical figures assume iconic and noble status infused with a higher calling of justice and democracy. Modern Americans embrace these caricatures as truth while carefully redacting history to retain only the most positive attributes. They imbue our founding with careful teaching of the Mayflower, Pilgrims, and religious freedoms. We frequently bounce from the founding of the Massachusetts Bay colony to the American Revolution, with little between the two events. Reality, however, involves a far more complicated situation, and many arrive in less-than-ideal situations. Large swaths of White Americans of English, Irish, and Scottish descent arrived here by force or in chains. Transported felons and indentured servants often had few rights.

Foundational Immigration

The involuntary immigrants to the American shores occurred for centuries. "Involuntary emigrants were those who were sent by authority of the government to serve for a term as a punishment in place of more severe penalties to which they were liable for offences committed" (Sollers, 1907, 19). The Carolinas, Virginia, and Maryland were frequent destinations for convicts sent to America. Eighteenth-century Britain had a population problem. The death penalty had grown increasingly unpopular during a period of social upheaval and growth. Transportation emerged by the eighteenth century as Britain's preferred punishment for noncapital offenses because "mass hangings or employments as chain gangs in England was considered barbaric and too politically risky" (Grubb, 2001, p. 295). London's lower-class population was growing, and the city could not keep up. Transportation offered an elegant solution to multiple concerns. The colonies needed labor on plantations to help harvest tobacco and other agricultural products. Britain had a growing population and crime problems with a mounting distaste for the death penalty. Removing convicts to the Americas became a solution that benefitted both sides from the British point of view. "In 1619, James I issued an order that certain vile and dissolute persons who swarmed the streets of London should be arrested and sent to Virginia" (Stillé, 1889, p. 460). "A certain sum was paid by the planters to secure the services of these convicts, or servants, as they were called for a fixed period, the term of their sentence and afterwards they were freemen" (Stillé, 1889, p. 461).

Many arrived either in chains or bound into labor to fulfill sentences passed by European courts. We often consider the only enslaved people on American shores to be from Africa. The harsh reality is vast numbers of White British citizens arrived in akin circumstances. Large numbers of White British citizens were transported into the colonies to serve time for crimes as transported felons or indentured servants. Legally, their rights were functionally indifferent to those of enslaved Africans in most cases. The colonies that created the United States were a medley of classes and social structures, all struggling to establish their place. Virginia law in 1748 was very clear about the general rights of convicts.

> AND whereas Convicts, as well as Negroes, Mulattoes, and Indians, are commonly of such corrupt Principles and their Testimony cannot be depended upon, to prevent such Mischiefs which may happen by admitting such precarious Evidence, Be it further enacted, by the Authority aforesaid, that no Person convicted and sentenced to Transportation, as is herein before recited, shall be admitted in any Court of this Colony, or before any Justice of Peace, to be sworn as a Witness, or give Evidence in any Cause, civil or criminal, except against or between any other Convicts, until the Term for which such Person was sentenced to be transported shall appear to be fully expired... (Hening, 1819, pp. 546–547)

There are many aspects to dissect within this statue. White convicts are structurally placed in the same social standing as chattel enslaved people, biracial persons, and Native Americans. All groups existed in the lowest rung of colonial American society. A convict was considered so base and corrupted that their testimony was inadmissible in court except against other convicts.

The importance here is not precisely the rights that were stripped but the view that convicts were considered a separate and minority class within American society. They were White but considered subordinate. These origins are, at best, superficially glanced over when discussing the founding of America. This country was populated by people England wanted to displace and remove from their populations.

> Convict servitude, in short, blurred the connections between place of birth, skin color, and freedom. Convicts were cheaper than 'white' slaves who made condition matter nearly as much as color in sorting out the

Chesapeake's social hierarchy. John Adams visited Baltimore in 1777 and concluded that the reliance on unfree labor had led 'Planters and Farmers to assume the title of Gentlemen, and they hold their Negroes and Convicts, that is all labouring People and Tradesmen, in such Contempt, that they think of themselves a distinct order of Beings'. (Bezis-Selfa, 2004, p. 87)

Convicts sent to Virginia were resented and treated as a separate settler class. Without guaranteed freedom dues, many, if not most, received nothing at the end of their sentence. These people created a class of Americans who lacked money and property in a society that required one, if not both, to vote and participate. These former convicts are often unable to return home either because of the threat of a death sentence upon return or simply lacking the ability to pay for their passage. "The ensuing crops of released convicts, like weeds, scattered their seed. Some of that seed settled down near the Potomac plantations, but some was blown far afield by the winds of fate and germinated on the new frontier beyond the Blue Ridge" (Harrison, 1922, p. 260).

Kercher (2003) describes the importance of felony attaint and how it applies to some convicts. "Attaint did not apply to all transported convicts, but only to those who had been sentenced to death and then received the king's conditional pardon of transportation" (p. 536). The death penalty sentence was more than just a formality in the British system. The person entered a living limbo where they were physically alive but dead in the eyes of the law. "At common law, they forfeited their goods to the Crown along with profits to their freehold land. They had no right to acquire further property, sue in the courts, or give evidence in court" (Kercher, 2003, p. 536). In Britain, these penalties were more significant to the heirs than the person if they were executed for their crimes. Criminal transportation added an additional wrinkle to the situation if they were sentenced to death but later given transportation instead of hanging. In that case, "a pardon conditional on transportation meant that the felon remained attainted until the period of transportation expired, then he or she had to live in the shadowy legal world for fourteen years or even more" (Kercher, 2003, p. 537). Attaint incentivized convicts to move where people may not know their backgrounds. "Even if it were known that a servant was a convict, unless there was proof of a death sentence having been imposed, the person could not be treated as attainted" (Kercher, 2003, p. 538). Attaint legally removed a person's rights to be a land owner, testify in court, or participate fully in society. American colonists were not as optimistic about the situation. Some of this disdain likely stems in part from the differences between them. Britain saw transportation as a redemptive act where criminals may "benefit as servants from the discipline of honest work, especially in the stark American wilderness" (Ekirch, 1987, p. 18). Americans saw the arrival of convicted felons as a way for Britain to dump their undesirables rather than unfortunates seeking the opportunity for salvation and reform.

> In 1718, by Act 4, George I, c. 2, the penalty (privilege) of transportation was extended to all felons sentenced to a term of imprisonment not less than three years; to return prior to the expiration of sentence was an offense punishable by death. ... For a time, four or five hundred were shipped to Maryland annually; others were sent to Virginia. The planters bought them. In effect, they were slaves, for a term of years; and the traffic in convicts was a form of competition with the African slave-trade. (Wines, 1919, pp. 168–169)

The population of the American colonies was growing at a rapid rate because of regular immigration from Europe. As with many places, population growth creates social pressures and raises crime and violence. The transported felon population became an easy scapegoat for these new burgeoning locales. Convict arrivals were considered the primary source for all instances of violent crimes and other felonies in the American colonies. The sheer number of these convicted British troubled many of the colonies. They passed local laws attempting to limit the numbers. Maryland, in 1723, had an act entitled "An Act to prevent the great evils arising by the importation of Convicts into the Provinces and for the better Discovery of such when imported" (Sollers, 1907, p. 29). Over time, convicts began to comprise larger and larger portions of colonial society. Morgan (1989) asserts that based on Richard Morris's (1946) numbers, convicts in Maryland were "more than a third of all immigrants into the province and nearly half of the indentured servants" (p. 254) between the years of 1745–1775. Both Morgan (1989) and Bailyn (1986) suggest "distinctions between convicts and indentured servants faded where labour needs were great in the Chesapeake" (Morgan, 1989, p. 257). The life of a convict servant in colonial America was harsh and brutal. Their physical appearance could cause suspicion. Many carried scars from irons secured around their necks or ankles or scars from diseases like smallpox that were caught upon ships or in other unhygienic prison situations (Morgan, 1989, p. 262).

> The new comers [referring to felons] included not only educated unfortunates like George Washington's first tutor and woman of Moll Flanders type, but degraded gin fiends, out of Hogarth's pictures and sturdy beggars. These last, after completing their stipulated seven years of plantation servitude and being forbidden to return to England, at the risk of being hands, became idle vagabonds in the colony. (Harrison, 1922, p. 252)

These populations were not insignificant. Campbell (1959) stated, "studies made in the last two decades have demonstrated that a far larger percentage of our colonial population entered the country under indenture than was formally thought. One-half of the total is held to be a conservative estimate" (p. 69). Someone else found that "When I said that two thirds of the persons now employed in Maryland in the instruction of youth were either indented servants or convicts, the assertion was not made quite at random, nor without as much previous authentic information as the nature of the case would admit of" (Boucher, 1797, p. 189). Ekirch (1987) asserted, "Transported convicts composed perhaps a quarter of British immigrants to colonial America during the eighteenth century" (p. 188).

The British took a dim view of the American colonies. Stillé (1889) recounted an English periodical that once suggested that Americans who were interested in their family histories "should be presented with a copy of the Newgate calendar as the truest record of the achievements of their forefathers" (p. 458). Newgate was the infamous British prison where many persons sentenced to transportation were held. Butler (1896) writes of an account recorded by Francis Lieber. Lieber, considered the first American political scientist, had a conversation in 1844 where he

> remarked how curious a fact it was that all American women look so genteel and refined, even the lowest; small heads, fine silky hair, delicate and marked eyebrows. [his English companion replied] Oh, that is easily accounted for. The super-abundance of public women, who are always rather good looking, were sent over to America in early times. (Butler, 1896, p. 12)

In other words, America was populated by prostitutes and other criminals transported over in abundance by Great Britain. The British considered most Americans the portions of their society they were happy to be rid of on their side of the Atlantic. There were planters, gentlemen, and other reputable persons, but the American colonies also took in their unwanted criminal poor. America was Australia before Australia. It was more accessible and convenient to ship people across the Atlantic than to the other side of the world. Australia did not open for the British as convict resettlement until 1789, or approximately the same year the United States ratified its current Constitution.

The United States, after this point, began a curious journey toward creating retroactive continuity about its founding. These indentured and transportation origins are downplayed in favor of a creation myth rife with Pilgrims and pumpkin pie. As we began to unify into a new nation and time moved on from the founding, we envisioned ourselves as a different people.

Immigration Moving Forward

The United States started thinking about qualifications for citizenship early into its existence. In 1790, it was established you had to live here for two years to become a citizen. It was raised to 5 years by 1795, and in 1798, we saw the Alien and Sedition Acts. There was fear of immigration swamping the United States from other places. With the Irish Rebellion of 1798 and the French Revolution, many foreigners came to America and created schools, newspapers, and other areas to gather. The Alien Acts were primarily seen as limiting rebellion and dissent rather than simply curtailing arrivals. American immigration began to shift in the 1820s with the start of the Industrial Revolution. We begin to see an uptick in immigration, which rapidly expanded in 1847 after the European potato famine.

American immigration and ideas about citizenship all begin to merge in the mid-nineteenth century. Many early British immigrants into America were believed to be of largely questionable character. Time and convenient social amnesia allowed their reinvention into long-standing Americans. Legacies of the dichotomy of these persons who arrived and cultivated their ancestral origins continue to exist. Americans, except for Indigenous Native Americans, are not Americans. They are descendants of other places around the world. Many have ancestries that originate within nationalities and ethnic groups. However, we have seen an emergence of people who consider themselves simply American within the United States. When asked, they do not mention ancestral ethnicities but refer to themselves as distinctly American. The ability to identify this group has been a relatively new phenomenon, though its existence is likely decades older.

To develop national, nativist pride, a considerable number of the American citizenry would have to slough off its older nationalities in favor of a unified one. It was a nation founded by a diverse population. Moreover, this population ranged from wealthy to poor. Vast numbers of poor Whites arrived as indentured or transported felons without the ability to return to their places of origin once their sentences ended. Early America placed strict limitations on participation, tying suffrage to residency, property ownership, and specific levels of wealth. Every colony had restrictions, though some were more restrictive than others (e.g., "Maryland, 1776;" "New Jersey, 1776;" "New York," 1777). All functioned as barriers to participation for the poor. As Americans moved West and South into the lands opened by Andrew Jackson's land removal policies in the 1830s, Whites moved into areas previously occupied by Native Americans. Many persons moving there likely, but not only were former transported felons, indentures, or their descendants. These populations found the developing states in these regions more open to land acquisition and had more friendly voting rights, with often few or few barriers found in most of the original states (e.g., "Alabama," n.d.; Littell, 1809).

American identity, thus, required a makeover. The distrusted and unwanted poor White castoffs from mostly Great Britain reinvented themselves in these new locales. They were no longer inferiors but equals within American society. With cheap land and suffrage, their identity under Jacksonian universal suffrage was electorally the same as wealthier Americas. These Americans transitioned from British unwanted to longstanding citizens who helped craft this nation. There are indications in the next several decades that help cement this identity. For example, the 1850 census was the first to ask whether a person was born inside or outside the United States. Their ancestral origins were asked if they were born outside the United States. Respondents born within the United States were not asked about their ancestral background. We see this growing identity associated with being a White American throughout the late nineteenth and early twentieth centuries. The immigration acts from the 1880s until 1965 reflect a society that considered the people already here different from more recent newcomers. These acts set up a situation where future immigration levels were based upon perceived previous ancestral immigration levels.

The Emergence of Americans

Though we do not have any data before 1980, we know a portion of the American population considers simply 'American' as their nationality. The 1980 census was the first that included an open-ended ancestral identity question. This question allowed "self-identification, provided no prelisted categories, and allowed for one or more ancestry responses" ("Ancestry," 1980, p. 1). Before the 1980 census, they only collected the "country of birth of persons and their parents and identified ethnicity for only foreign-born native persons of foreign or mixed parentage" ("Ancestry," 1980, p. 1). A non-insignificant percentage of White people indicated their ancestral origins were 'American' surprising researchers. The report from the census reads somewhat dismissive. "Although respondents were instructed to provide a response which referred to their nationality group, lineage, or country in which they or their ancestors were born before their arrival in the United States, 13.3 million persons (or 6 percent) wrote in a single response of 'American' or 'United States'" ("Ancestry," 1980, p. 6). The report continued by noting that the "South also had the largest proportion of the population reporting 'American' or 'United States' (9 percent) or that did not report any ancestry (14 percent)" ("Ancestry," 1980, p. 1). Other researchers looked into these quirky ancestral results and found they were clustered among the less educated and pastoral areas of Appalachia and the South (Farley, 1991, p. 415; Fuguitt et al., 1989, p. 150; Lieberson & Waters, 1993, p. 431) whose families immigrated before the Civil War and in many cases, likely before 1800 (Fuguitt et al., 1989, p. 150; Lieberson & Waters, 1993, p. 423). When religiosity was examined, they were primarily evangelical low-church Protestants (Arbour & Teigen, 2011). The results of the 1980 census could be dismissed as a categorical idiosyncrasy. However, the group remained in subsequent censuses and even showed growth. Though not definitive, these results hint at the fact these people may be descendants of indentures, transported felons, and others who felt abandoned by their home country on colonial shores. They forged new identities in the United States, casting off their historical baggage and embracing identities as simply Americans.

The 1990 census demonstrated this rural, evangelical American population was relatively stable at 12.4 million ("Ancestry: 2000," 2000, p. 3). The 2000 census allowed for multiple ancestral origins. They implemented this change because of concerns that individuals of numerous ancestries indicated they were Americans out of convenience. Instead, Americans grew to 20.2 million, or 7.2 percent of the total population, which was any group's most significant absolute numerical growth during the previous ten years. ("Ancestry: 2000," 2000, p. 3). This stable trend continued in the 2010 collection. The 2013 five-year estimates from the American Community Survey indicate that 20,200,882 persons out of 311,536,594, or 6.48 percent, indicated that their ancestry was 'American' ("First Ancestry Reported," 2013). These 'Americans' represent an organized, stable portion of the population. Their identities are unique and durable, and they have cohesive ideas about the government's responsibility to the people. Assuming this ancestral identification is accurate, it makes logical sense data suggests this population trends toward individualism and suspicion of authority (Knoll, 2016, p. 678). Attitudes are passed over the dinner table, generation after generation. While the details may be lost, the emotions of a British government removing them from their shores, followed by dismissal from an American one favoring its upper classes, likely lingered across time.

The identity of these Americans has intriguing implications. If a stable population sees themselves as simply 'Americans' from 1980 onward, it is logical to assume they held a similar identity before that time. The 1980 census inadvertently picked up on the effect, but it demonstrated that a significant percentage of White Americans claimed the United States as their ancestral heritage. If a White 'American' identity conflates with ancestral origins, then restrictive immigration policies would seem logical.

Restrictive Immigration Policies

We do see the beginning of restrictive immigration policies in 1882. There are two significant actions this year that impact immigration. The first and more infamous is the Chinese Exclusion Act. This legislation "excluded all Chinese laborers from immigration to the United States for a period of ten years" (Wright, 2008, p. 58). The second was the Act of Regulate Immigration. This act provided for the "exclusion of 'convicts, lunatics, idiots, and those liable to become a public charge'" (Wright, 2008, p. 59). The Chinese Exclusion Act in 1882 targeted one specific nationality against immigration, but as we move into the twentieth century, laws barring immigration become more broad. The 1891 Immigration Act allows for the exclusion of the insane, paupers, people with contagious diseases, people convicted of moral turpitude crimes, and also idiots. By 1892, rights toward those of Chinese ancestral origins were constrained even further. The Geary Act kept Chinese exclusion in place and required resident permits to be carried at all times. "Congress stated that 'any Chinese person or person of Chinese descent' was deemed to be in the country illegally unless he or she could demonstrate otherwise" (Wright, 2008, p. 67). According to Wright (2008), this act "tried to make any Chinese person as near a non-person as possible" (p. 67), and, though challenged in court, the Supreme Court did uphold these restrictions. When the renewal of these Chinese exclusion came up for renewal again in 1902, they were renewed, but the ten-year limit was removed, allowing for indefinite exclusion. It would remain in force until 1943 when a small number of Chinese were allowed to immigrate annually in recognition of our mutual allied status in the Second World War (Wright, 2008, p. 74).

The 1907 Immigration Act excludes:

> All idiots, imbeciles, feebleminded persons, epileptics, insane persons, and persons who have been insane within five years previous; persons who have had two or more attacks of insanity at any time previously; paupers; persons likely to become a public charge; professional beggars; persons afflicted with tuberculosis or with a loathsome or dangerous contagious disease; persons not comprehended within any of the foregoing excluded classes who are found to be and are certified by the examining surgeon as being mentally or physically defective, such mental or physical defect being of a nature which may affect the ability of such alien to earn a living; persons who have been convicted of or admit having committed a felony or other crime or misdemeanor involving moral turpitude; polygamists, or persons who admit their belief in the practice of polygamy, anarchists... ("Immigration Act, " n.d.; Hutchinson, 1981)

The 1907 Expatriation Act removed American citizenship from any American woman who married a man who did not hold American citizenship. This removal was immediate and without notification. Citizenship followed men, not women. Foreign women who married American men were automatically granted citizenship. American women would continue to lose their citizenship in this manner until the 1922 Cable Act. Tying citizenship to nationality almost certainly functioned as a way to dissuade American women from marrying outside of their nationality. It fits within the overall concept of Americanization of a national identity. Ten years later, the 1917 Immigration Act extended restrictions within an Asiatic Barred Zone defined by latitude and longitude. It included Afghanistan, Arabia, India, the USSR east of the Ural Mountains, Burma, Thailand, most Polynesian Islands, and China, but did exclude the Philippines and Japan. A literacy test for those allowed was implemented, and certain professions were also immune from the exclusion (Wright, 2008). These exclusions would not be removed until 1952.

Congress had grappled with immigration issues long before the act's passage in 1920. They had brought in Harry Laughlin, a noted eugenicist, to present "an expert report to Congress, 'Biological Aspects of Immigration,' on April 16, 1920" (Chase, 1977, p. 291). Harry Laughlin was appointed the "Expert Eugenics Agent on the House Committee on Immigration and Naturalization" (Chase, 1977, p. 289) by chairman Albert Johnson. As the congressional expert, Laughlin conducted research from 1921 to 1931, and it was published by the Government Printing Office (Wright, 2008, p. 85). Albert Johnson, one of the sponsors of the Johnson-Reed Act, also known as the Immigration Act of 1924, was also the chairman of the House Committee on Immigration and Naturalization since 1919. Albert Johnson was also "installed as the president of the Eugenics Research Association in 1923" (Chase, 1977, p. 289). During this presentation, Laughlin notes that experts at the Eugenics Records Office to that day had "failed to find a case in history in which two races have lived side by side for a number of generations and have maintained racial purity" (Chase, 1977, p. 293). He also stated as fact that "immigration and native moronic and imbecile women were not only more promiscuous but also more fertile than respectable Nordic-American ladies of good stock" (Chase, 1977, p. 293). The purpose of these comments is fearmongering for the restriction of immigration along with the pursuit of eugenic goals of sterilization, containment, and racial purity. Laughlin maintains racial intermixing will inevitably occur when any two groups live near each other in a region.

Lothrop Stoddard and Madison Grant were influential in developing restrictive immigration policies in the early twentieth century. Both could likely be best described as racial philosophers. They did early social science work and examined scientific racism to make their cases. However, while superficially appearing rigorous, their work largely hinges upon their readings and personal perspectives on the development of civilizations. Large swaths of human history get compressed into their readings to craft tales that framed Western European Whites as the saviors and utmost expression of superior development within civilization. Social and biological commingle to the point of meaninglessness because standards fluctuate depending upon the idea being pushed forward at the moment. Stoddard (1920) in *The Rising Tide of Color Against White World Supremacy*, was highly influential in pressing his case for immigration limitations. He asserted the "admission of aliens should, indeed, be regarded just as solemnly as the begetting of children, for the racial effect is essentially the same" (Stoddard, 1920, p. 252). He said, "You cannot make bad stock into good by changing its meridian" (Stoddard, 1920, p. 258). He also strongly disagreed with racial mixing, saying, "the children of such cross-breeding are liable to inherit two souls, two temperaments, two sets of opinions" and uses Cuba, Mexico, and Brazil as his exemplar cases (Stoddard, 1920, p. 259). He argues the fundamental character of a person merges with their nativity. Children produced from multicultural backgrounds stand apart as neither.

His narrow perspective is on full display when he discusses the founding of the United States. He says, "Probably few persons fully appreciate what magnificent racial treasures America possessed at the beginning of the nineteenth century. The colonial sock was perhaps the finest that nature had evolved since the classic Greeks" (Stoddard, 1920, p. 261). Stoddard's focus on racial purity defined immigration qualities in that he either was completely ignorant or bluntly ignored the indentured servant and transported felon origins of much colonial American immigration. He wanted to stop immigration to the United States from most places. He asserted that "the immigrant tide must at all costs be stopped and American given the chance to stabilize her ethnic being" (Stoddard, 1920, p. 266). Stoddard's beliefs were, at that time, well-received and respected. He wrote multiple works and framed immigration as an encroaching threat upon the United States.

> The rise of the New American has, however, had one rather startling result: it has roused the Old American. Shocked broad awake, the old stock is for the first time developing a real racial consciousness. Hitherto the average American's racial vision did not extend much beyond a perception of such obvious racial differences as those which separated him from the negro, the

Red Indian, or the Mongolian of Eastern Asia. Now, however, he is fast realizing that 'America' means not only certain ideals and institutions but also a racial stock, which must be preserved if the ideals and institutions which that stock has created are to endure. To the New American's cry that America is still 'in the making,' and that it should become a hybrid civilization, the Old American answers grimly that America is basically " made " -and that it shall not be unmade. (Stoddard, 1924, p. 243)

Stoddard also testified in front of Congress about these policies. In January 1924, he was considered an expert witness about potential immigration groups (Chase, 1977, pp. 293–294). Both Lothrop Stoddard and Madison Grant's work was used to justify why particular groups, such as people of Jewish ancestry, were problematic for the racial composition of the United States. According to Chase (1977), "It is impossible to overestimate the impact of Laughlin's report [about Army IQ tests] ... on Congress and the nation" (p. 298). Hiram Wesley Evans, leader or Imperial Wizard of the Klu Klux Klan from 1922–1939, was highly complimentary toward Laughlin, noting his testimony "for the Committee on Immigration as remarkable study of the relative degeneracy of all classes of social inadequates except the venereal" (Chase, 1977, p. 300). To set quotas for the intake of populations, the United States also had to determine the general ancestry of persons on its soil. Joseph A. Hill was the person at the Census Bureau chairing the committee that set the quotas.

> One of the most serious problems he confronted was the lack of reliable information about the national origins of the white native-stock population. Hill deduced that roughly half the white population in 1920 consisted of descendants from the original colonial population, but the census of 1790 did not record data on place of birth. (Ngai, 1999 p. 78)

Census did a study in 1909 where they looked at surnames, which they used to help formulate those numbers. Ngai (1999) points out this is highly suspicious, even to Hill, "because it failed to recognize that some names were common to more than one country and that many Irish and German names had been anglicized" (p. 78).

The Immigration Act of 1924 was considered necessary to extend some of the restrictions by the Emergency Immigration Act of 1921. This 1921 act "restricted the number of aliens allowed entry to 3% of each nationality resident in the U.S. in 1910" (Massey, 2016, p. 21).

In other words, they used the nationality percentages from the 1910 census to calculate immigration allowances. "The Emergency Quota Act of 1921 became the basis of American immigration policy that lasted until the 1960s. The 3 percent quota stipulated in the 1921 act was subsequently reduced through the Quota Act of 1924" (Murphy, 2012). The 1921 act was touted to help control population surges following the First World War. The 1924 act, however, further reduced these numbers to just 2 percent and also moved the baselines off the 1910 census and onto the 1890 one to intentionally lower the allowable numbers. Ngai (1999) asserts, "The Immigration Act of 1924 contributed to the racialization of immigrant groups around notions of whiteness, permanent foreignness, and illegality" (p. 92). People of European origins frequently began to be termed just White, whereas other groups got hyphens to be permanently reminded of their 'other' origins. This act essentially banned most immigration from Asia and placed heavy restrictions on national origins.

On December 6, 1923, President Calvin Coolidge gave his first annual message. It was the first radio speech to be broadcast by a president to the entire nation. Within this speech, he said, "America must be kept American" ("December 6," n.d.). Calvin Coolidge threw his support behind calls for strong immigration restrictions. "The lines drawn in 1924 also helped change the conceptions of 'race,' particularly defining 'whiteness' more exclusively" (Yuill, 2021, p. 83). Much of the framing of modern immigration at the United States southern border can find its roots extending from the 1924 Immigration Act. "Within days of the passage of the 1924 Immigration Act, Congress created the Border Patrol to police migrants' movement along the borders, and in 1929 passed the Undesirable Aliens Act to control and criminalize Mexican migration" (Marinari, 2022, p. 277). The 1924 act implemented a quota system that heavily favored Northern and Western Europeans. Chase (1977), points out that in one year, "the number of immigrants from Italy had fallen 83 percent; the number of immigrants from Russia, Poland, and Central and Eastern Europe … were down by an average 83 percent; even Great Britain… suffered a 54 percent drop in immigrants from 1924 and 1925" (p. 300). "It still allowed an average of 287,000 immigrants per year to enter during the late twenties, chiefly, because it continued the exemption of Canada and Latin American countries from the quota system" (Higham, 1968, p. 324). It is essential to point out that "after 1927, a total quota of 150,000 would be parceled out in ratio to the distributions of national origins in the white population of the United States in

1920" (Higham, 1968, p. 324). These immigration restrictions all aim to keep out populations that are considered unacceptable. Social, ethnic, and racial purity were the ambitions of the authors of this legislation. The United States had to craft itself in an image consistent with American patriotic purity ideals. Border control was not just about keeping people out but keeping desirables within the population. Exclusions, whether they manifest as literal containment at the border, refusal of entry, or banned nationalities, all center around concepts of spatial segregation. Spatial segregation means you place space or distance between groups. This sort of expanse also means populations cannot come into contact with each other.

Isolating groups results in persons not mingling or interacting in social or public settings. When people interact, some are invariably often attracted to each other, and they may start dating. If that is successful, they may ultimately marry and have children. For persons who advocate against racial suicide, non-restricted immigration runs the risk of thwarting your goals. Eugenicists aimed for the best persons, believing that specific ethnicities, usually Northern and Western White Europeans, held the best genetic potential for greatness. Miscegenation and sterilization laws aim to prevent the dilution of idealized genetic stocks. Immigration bans and barriers attempt to achieve the same goals but prevent the introduction of said dilution. These beliefs were widespread and mainstream. The Director of Vital Statistics at the Bureau of Statistics for the State of Virginia wrote in 1928,

> The great mistake of introducing Negroes, and the danger of their presence in the most intimate relations with the whites … A number of cases have been called to my attention of apparent reversion, children of marked Negroid characteristics being born, when both parents are supposed to be pure white… Can a more humiliating occurrence be imagined for a white women of refined sensibilities? (Gejman & Weilbaecher, 2002, p. 227)

Proctor (1988), when discussing the Third Reich in Germany, states that "racial scientists were also impressed with American's 1924 Immigration Restriction Laws and the anti-miscegenation laws" (p. 100). He had also noted how these German officials were impressed with our sterilization and racial theories about purity. Fritz Lens, a German geneticist and one of their leading eugenicists cited Laughlin's "view that a proper sterilization effort in the United States would encompass 100,000 individuals in the first few years, rising to 400,000 a year by 1980 ... [and] approximately 15 million individuals of inferior race stock by 1980" (Proctor, 1988, p. 99).

Conclusion

The importance of the 1924 Immigration Act cannot be understated. Eugenic nativist appeals were presented as factual evidence to curtail further immigration from many places around the globe. Older immigrant groups were reframed as populations under attack at a fundamental cellular level. Immigration restrictions became tools of safety, security, and protection rather than artifacts of racial or ethnic biases. Sinister motives were imposed upon potential immigrant groups by others determined to keep them out of the United States. Eugenicists envisioned an America where immigration was only afforded to the worthiest, but your ancestry and not your accomplishment determined that standard. They also wanted to impose a caste system within the United States where persons considered our best could populate the country. Persons considered lesser would often be regulated, such as livestock, with sterilization programs to facilitate fiscal responsibility from a social welfare perspective. These ideas were widespread and crept into the American conscience as factual perspectives. Later immigration acts, such as the ones in 1965 and 1990, drastically increased immigration but were defined to the American public as measures of equality and equity. These restrictions passed in the 1920s and remained our defining immigration policy for forty years. The biased roots of these actions cast a long shadow upon the American public. The language used and deployed in this era has been routinely recycled or even upcycled over the years, especially during the presidential campaigns and administration of Donald Trump. The tone, intention, and overarching goal of many of Trump's immigration policies find their roots in the actions of eugenic immigration goals from the late nineteenth and early twentieth centuries.

References

Alabama: Constitution of 1819. (n.d.). *The Avalon Project.* https://avalon.law.yale.edu/19th_century/ala1819.asp

Ancestry of the Population by State: 1980, Supplementary Report. (1980). *1980 Census of the Population*. U.S. Census Bureau, U.S. Department of Commerce.

Ancestry: 2000. (2000). *Census 2000 Brief*. U.S. Census Bureau, U.S. Department of Commerce.

Arbour, B. K., & Teigen, J. M. (2011). Barack Obama's 'American' Problem: Unhyphened Americans in the 2008 Elections. *Social Science Quarterly, 92*(3), 563–587.

Bailyn, B. (1986). *Voyagers to the West: Emigration from Britain to America on the Eve of the Revolution*. Knopf.

Bezis-Selfa, J. (2004). *Forging America: Ironworkers, Adventurers, and the Industrious Revolution*. Cornell University Press.

Boucher, J. (1797). *A View of the Causes and Consequences of the American Revolution*. G.G. and J. Robinson.

Butler, J. D. (1896). British Convicts Shipped to American Colonies. *The American Historical Review, 2*(1), 12–33.

Campbell, M. (1959). Social Origins of Some Early Americans. In J. M. Smith (Ed.), *Seventeenth-Century America: Essays in Colonial History* (pp. 63–89). University of North Carolina Press.

Chase, A. (1977). *The Legacy of Malthus: The Social Costs of the New Scientific Racism*. Random House.

December 6, 1923: First Annual Message. (n.d.). *Presidential Speeches UVA Miller Center*. https://millercenter.org/the-presidency/presidential-speeches/december-6-1923-first-annual-message

Ekirch, A. R. (1987). *Bound for America: The Transportation of British Convicts to the Colonies 1718–1775*. Clarendon Press.

Farley, R. (1991). The New Census Question about Ancestry: What Did It Tell Us? *Demography, 28*(3), 411–429.

First Ancestry Reported. (2013). *American Community Survey*. U.S. Census Bureau, U.S. Department of Commerce.

Fuguitt, G. V., Brown, D. L., & Beale, C. L. (1989). *Rural and Small Town America*. Russell Sage Foundation.

Gejman, P. V., & Weilbaecher, A. (2002). History of the Eugenics Movement. *Israel Journal of Psychiatry and Related Sciences, 39*(4), 217–231.

Grubb, F. (2001). The Market Evaluation of Criminality: Evidence from the Auction of British Convict Labor in America, 1767–1775. *The American Economic Review, 91*(1), 295–304.

Harrison, F. (1922). When the Convicts Came: A Chapter from "Land Marks of Old Prince William." *The Virginia Magazine of History and Biography, 30*(3), 250–260.

Hening, W. W. (1819). *Laws of Virginia October 1748 22nd George II" The Statutes at Large; Being a Collection of All the Laws of Virginia* (Vol. 5). Franklin Press.

Higham, J. (1968). *Strangers in the Land: Patters of American Nativism, 1860–1925*. Atheneum Paperbacks.

Hutchinson, E. P. (1981). *Legislative History of American Immigration Policy, 1798–1965*. University of Pennsylvania Press.

Immigration Act 1907. (n.d.). *History Central*. https://www.historycentral.com/documents/immigrationact.html

Kercher, B. (2003). Perish or Prosper: The Law and Convict Transportation in the British Empire, 1700–1850. *Law and History Review, 21*(3), 527–584.

Knoll, B. R. (2016). The Political Behavior of 'Unhyphenated Americans:' An Individual-Level Analysis of Causes and Consequences. *Social Science Quarterly, 97*(3), 668–681.

Lieberson, S., & Waters, M. C. (1993). The Ethnic Responses of Whites: What Causes Their Instability, Simplification, and Inconsistency? *Social Forces, 72*(2), 421–450.

Littell, W. (1809). First Constitution for the State of Kentucky. *The Statute Law of Kentucky* (Vol. 1). William Hunter.

Marinari, M. (2022). The 1921 and 1924 Immigration Acts a Century Later: Roots and Long Shadows. *The Journal of American History, 109*(2), 271–283.

Maryland, Constitution of. (1776, November 11). *The Avalon Project*. https://avalon.law.yale.edu/17th_century/ma02.asp

Massey, C. G. (2016). Immigration Quotas and Immigrant Selection. *Explorations in Economic History, 60*, 21–40.

Morgan, K. (1989). Convict Runaways in Maryland, 1745–1775. *Journal of American Studies, 23*(2), 252–268.

Morris, R. B. (1946). *Government and Labor in Early America*. Columbia University Press.

Murphy, T. (2012). Emergency Quota Act of 1921. In W. R. Miller (Ed.), *The Social History of Crime and Punishment in America: An Encyclopedia* (Vol. 5, p. 537). Sage Publications, Inc.

New Jersey, Constitution of. (1776). *The Avalon Project*. https://avalon.law.yale.edu/18th_century/nj15.asp

New York, Constitution of. (1777, April 20). *The Avalon Project*. https://avalon.law.yale.edu/18th_century/ny01.asp

Ngai, M. M. (1999). The Architecture of Race in American Immigration Law: A Reexamination of the Immigration Act of 1924. *The Journal of American History, 86*(1), 67–92.

Proctor, R. N. (1988). *Racial Hygiene: Medicine Under the Nazis*. Harvard University Press.

Sollers, B. (1907). Transported Convict Laborers in Maryland during the Colonial Period. *Maryland Historical Magazine, II*(1), 17–47.

Stillé, C. J. (1889). American Colonies as Penal Settlements. *The Pennsylvania Magazine of History and Biography, 12*(4), 457–464.

Stoddard, L. (1920). *The Rising Tide of Color Against White World-Supremacy.* Charles Scribner's Sons.

Stoddard, L. (1924). *Racial Realities in Europe.* Charles Scribner's Sons.

Wines, F. H. (1919). *Punishment and Reformation: A Study of the Penitentiary System.* Thomas Y. Cromwell Company.

Wright, R. O. (2008). *Chronology of Immigration in the United States.* McFarland & Co.

Yuill, K. (2021). "America must remain American": The Liberal Contribution to Race Restrictions in the 1924 Immigration Act. *Federal History.* Downloaded from: http://sure.sunderland.ac.uk/id/eprint/13154/

CHAPTER 4

Donald Trump's Rhetoric and How Eugenics Frames His World

Abstract This chapter examines specific statements and quotes Donald Trump made as a presidential candidate and sitting president. These are contextualized and compared with language, phrases, and classic, influential writings by early twentieth-century eugenicists. The chapter discusses the difference between the rights of a citizen versus a subject and how many eugenic policies and Donald Trump's positions make distinctions between the two groups. This chapter looks at Trump's words regarding immigration, abortion policy, health, fitness, and religion, as well as other areas, comparing and pointing out similarities to early advocates of eugenics and others who bemoaned race suicide. The chapter also explores many slurs and derisive monikers Donald Trump attaches to other people. There is a clear delineation of how he addresses people negatively. Women of color receive intentional, personalized, targeted language, often assigning alliterative terms that dog whistle as well as demean. The chapter shows how Donald Trump's language and rhetoric are not innovative but heavily draw upon others' ideas to evoke strong connections to America's eugenic past.

Keywords Donald Trump · Eugenics · Citizen versus subject · Immigration · Slurs

© The Author(s), under exclusive license to Springer Nature Switzerland AG 2024
S. B. O'Brien, *Eugenics in American Political Life*,
https://doi.org/10.1007/978-3-031-63553-3_4

Most of us are tempted to handwave away thoughts of eugenics as an unfortunate part of the past. We disconnect our present from the past, absolving us of the responsibility of understanding how eugenics still shapes our world today. Words, phrases, and attitudes of our current lives still have elements of aspects from previous generations. Eugenics has also emerged as a boogeyman to point fingers in the direction of one or two people in an attempt to absolve everyone else. Eugenics was a movement that was embraced by large swaths of the entire public. It was not isolated. It was not niche. Many of their ideas are still with us, albeit rebranded into other packages. If you put a McDonald's burger in a Burger King wrapper, it is still a McDonald's burger. The core heart and soul of Western eugenics continues through today. Donald Trump, in particular, utilizes rhetoric, political attitudes, and stereotypes commonplace in the early to mid-twentieth-century eugenics movement.

The words and actions of Donald Trump and his administration's policies strongly suggest eugenic rationales were an integral part of his presidency. The words and thoughts of the early eugenics researchers echo within this administration's objectives for immigration. They show themselves in the speeches of Donald Trump over decades, before, during, and after his presidential administration. Donald Trump's rhetoric parrots much of the Eugenic Movement's beliefs and worldviews almost a century later. Through understanding the origins, development, variety, and depth of eugenics within American life in the past, we can better understand how it is still shaping our world today. From personal to political policies, Trump engages with the world via this lens to justify and ballast many thoughts and positions. Donald Trump's 2016 run for the presidency and subsequent election was unique for various reasons. His statements, 'dog whistles,' claims, and attitudes toward immigration and non-Whites surprised large sections of twenty-first-century America. Many were also bewildered by the deep levels of support Donald Trump found within many White communities within the United States, especially among evangelical Protestants (Smith, 2024). Trump resonated with specific groups of men who responded well to appeals of unabashedly masculine attitudinal positions (Carian & Sobotka, 2018). The American Eugenics movement and its various bedfellows, like Muscular Christianity, help explain Trump's appeal in several ways.

Donald Trump appears to be a careful student or raised within an environment that instilled eugenics concepts as acceptable. His father, Fred Trump, had a history of racial discrimination in his real estate properties. Woody Guthrie wrote a song entitled 'Old Man Trump' that discussed Fred Trump's discriminatory racial policies in his housing projects (Kaufman, 2016). The Justice Department in the 1970s was involved in a lawsuit with the Trumps over their discriminatory policies, which was eventually settled but not dismissed or acquitted (Barnett, 1979; Mahler & Eder, 2016). There has also been persistent speculation of Fred Trump's involvement with the Klu Klux Klan following an arrest in the 1920s (Ayers, 2021; Brockell, 2023; Martinez, 2017). He was arrested at a rally but released. His direct involvement was never proven or disproven, but all men arrested "were represented by the same lawyers" (Brockell, 2023).

Genetic Superiority

Donald Trump has often brought up his superior genes, likely because "Fred Trump... taught him that the family's success was genetic" (Mortimer, 2016). At a Minnesota September 18, 2020 campaign rally, Donald Trump said, "You have good genes, you know that, right? You have good genes. A lot of it is about the genes, isn't it, don't you believe? The racehorse theory. You think we're so different? You have good genes in Minnesota" (Mehta, 2020; "Trump said," 2020). These comments matter because many Scandinavians and Germans heavily settled in that part of the United States in Minnesota. In particular, Swedish and Norwegians significantly influenced that state's development (Lintelman, 2019; Nickel, 2021). Eugenicists routinely hold Scandinavian, and in particular, Norwegian ancestry, as the epitome of racial excellence. Harry Laughlin, who authored many of America's fundamental eugenics laws and was also awarded by the Third Reich for his work, stated in 1922 U.S. House of Representative hearings about immigration that "As a rule, we get good immigrants from Norway" (Laughlin, 1922, p. 756) as well as stating "our finest and most desirable immigrants" (Laughlin, 1922, p. 755) come from there as well. Minnesota has one of America's highest percentages of Norwegian ancestry, 13.3%, second only to North Dakota at 22.5% (Norwegian Population by State, 2024).

These ideals of Nordic supremacy were common among prominent eugenicists of the early twentieth century. Madison Grant was one of their most active advocates, authoring the book *The Passing of the Great Race* in 1916. His works helped shape American laws against interracial marriage and immigration and were frequently cited by the Third Reich.

Madison Grant, in the introduction of Lothrop Stoddard's book, *The Rising Tide of Color: The Threat Against White World-Supremacy*, wrote, "Democratic ideals among an homogenous population of Nordic blood, as in England or America, is one thing, but it is quite another for the white man to share his blood with, or intrust his ideals to, brown, yellow, black or red men" (Stoddard, 1920, p. xxxii). These words still matter because they shape attitudes that see people as race and ethnicity rather than individuals. Madison Grant and Lothrop Stoddard consider Nordics "The Great Race" (Stoddard, 1920, p. 162), claiming that they improve every civilization they mingle with among other Whites. However, they believe other racial groups degrade societies that are racially, ethnically, and culturally integrated. Social situations and political stability were intertwined with race. Any criticisms or rebuttals could be justified away with dismissive language of unique situations, while supportive information was always relevant and incontrovertible. Lothrop Stoddard (1924), in *Racial Realities in Europe*, stated,

> The United States was founded by men of Nordic stock; its institutions, ideals, and culture are typical fruits of the Nordic spirit. These are the things which make 'America.' Yet only so long as America remains predominantly Nordic in blood will these things endure. History shows conclusively that as the blood of a nation changes, so does every phase of the national life; it proves beyond the shadow of a doubt that if the United States should cease to be a mainly Nordic land, our America would pass away. (Stoddard, 1924, p. 239)

In 2018, President Trump was unhappy about immigrants from Haiti, El Salvador, and Africa and reportedly said, "Why are we having all these people from shithole countries come here" (Dawsey, 2018)? He "then suggested that the United States should instead bring more people from countries such as Norway" (Dawsey, 2018). He initially claimed he did not say it (Jackson, 2018) but later refused to deny it when given a chance (Haltiwanger, 2018). While several officials had no comment, Senator Dick Durban confirmed it was spoken ("How it happened," 2018). This language mirrors the rhetoric of eugenicists who placed a high value on these ancestries, so much so that it was referred to as American Nordicist (or Nordicism) racial ideology (Kohlman, 2014). Nordicism was behind the substantial quota restriction in the Johnson-Reed/Immigration Act of 1924, giving oversized preference to Northwestern European immigration while substantially curtailing every other region.

Donald Trump has also often attributed his success to his German blood and genetic superiority (Chait, 2020; Kahn et al., 2020). Trump has made statements alluding to his belief that bloodlines convey excellence. "During his campaign, he told CNN: 'I had an uncle who went to MIT who is a top professor. Dr. John Trump. A genius. It's in my blood. I'm smart'" (Kranish, 2020). Donald Trump is proud of his family lineage and believes it gives him an intellectual advantage. He attained genius by birthright, not hard work or personal education. Scholars of eugenic race culture believe genius lies within heredity. Caleb Saleeby (1909) states, "it is impossible to question that heredity transmission of genius or great talent does occur" (p. 289). He uses the Bach family, Thomas and Matthew Arnold, and James and John Stuart Mill as exemplars, highlighting how genius must have been passed from Erasmus Darwin to his children to create such genius first cousins in Charles Darwin and Francis Galton (Saleeby, 1909, pp. 289–290).

Donald Trump appears to be an ardent advocate of scientific racism. In a September 29, 2020 debate, "'You could never have done the job we did,' Trump said to former Vice President Joe Biden, the Democratic nominee. 'You don't have it in your blood'" (Mehta, 2020). These comments are more than just innocuous debating. Joe Biden has English, Scottish, and Irish ancestry but is most notably known for his Irish roots. Irish have long been disparaged as inferior to other European ethnic groups. In the 1860s, Cambridge professor Charles Kingsley referred to the Irish as 'human chimpanzees,' others denigrated them to highlight their lack of Anglo-Saxon roots (Quinn, 1995). More importantly, Trump's comments are likely also a subtle attack upon Biden's religion. The Catholic church opposed the Eugenics Movement in the early twentieth century (Leon, 2013). In 1912, Harvard's president emeritus, Charles William Eliot, gave a speech in which he did not oppose immigration per se but any race mixing that may result. In particular, he warned about Irish Catholics marrying Anglo-Saxon Protestants (Cohen, 2016). Donald Trump's attempts to intentionally disparage Biden's blood strike at the heart of anti-Catholic and anti-Irish sentiments that ran rife through the Eugenics Movement. He openly claims that Biden's Irish ancestry places him at a disadvantage that should function as a disqualifier.

These comments and statements echo many of the similar phrases utilized by eugenicists decades earlier, though they would more commonly use terms like 'fit and unfit.' Racehorse theory mentioned by Donald Trump refers to breeding principles where better stock is created by matching two prime examples of thoroughbreds. It is explicitly why many eugenicists wanted to regulate marriages and pushed for the banning of interracial marriages. Lindsay (1998) points out, "When 'nationhood' was reformulated as national heredity, the eugenic marriage law represented, in effect, a strategy of national self-constitution" (p. 571). Marriage to produce children represents the future of the family and the survival of the best possible population for a country. Dilution of strong stock with fewer genetic options means weakening a country as a whole for adherents of these belief systems. Earnest Cox (1923) writes in *White America* that race mixing would destroy White civilization. He was one of the supporters who "in 1924 convinced the General Assembly to pass the Virginia Act to Preserve Racial Integrity, probably the nation's strictest anti-miscegenation statute" (Smith, 2020). Cox believed "the white race, as white, has outdistanced the other races in cultural attainments, spiritual and material" (Cox, 1925, p. 24). The edition this author used for research was a March 1925 'Special Reprint for Distribution to Members of Congress' which means it was given out to the U.S. Congress as they were working to refine the Johnson-Reed Act's immigration provisions. His claims throughout the book center around variations on his theme of "the more Caucasian the people the more civilized the country" (Cox, 1925, p. 201). In his view, Latin America is deeply flawed, and its only hope for salvation is heavy White immigration from North America and Europe (Cox, 1925, p. 202). Harry Laughlin, during his November 21, 1922, testimony in front of the House of Representatives Committee on Immigration and Naturalization, was looking at population quotas, health, and labor situations. "In analyzing social and racial conditions and outlooks, if the South has its negro problem, the rest of the United States has the immigrant problem" (Laughlin, 1922, p. 745). Less than 20 days later, albeit over in the Senate, the Mammy statue bill was introduced during this same session of Congress. The issues of race, immigration, and supremacy are linked together to help craft a vision of an idealized, curated America hallmarked by White hegemony.

In *The Revolt against Civilization: the Menace of the Under Man* (1922), Lothrop Stoddard wanted people to understand that degenerates were not necessarily inferior. Stoddard wanted to reconcile White degenerates with his overall view of supremacy. More bluntly, he was trying to reframe the discussion because, in his view, Whites could be degenerate but not inferior. Racial and ethnic minorities could be degenerate as well as inferior. Stoddard was unhappy with how degenerate and inferior were conflating as synonyms, particularly in immigration debates. Whites, by their nature, could never be inferior, and the synonym was, in its way, equalizing Whites and other races. He wanted to separate inferior and degenerate by creating a new word, under-man. He tried to popularize the idea of the under-man, or "the man who measures under the standard of capacity and adaptability improved by the social order in which he lives" (Stoddard, 1922, p. 23). Stoddard's ideas heavily influenced the Third Reich, and based on this book, the term 'Untermensch' was incorporated into their society. Stoddard's terminology was used and employed by Heinrich Himmler in a pamphlet labeled under this term. It called Russians part of this under-man and all persons of Jewish ancestry (Muller & Ueberschar, 2002, p. 245). These ideas are key because people frequently point to the Third Reich as the creator of these terms when they originated within the United States. Stoddard's ideas were so well-received in Hitler's Germany that he was allowed to go to and write a travel book about his experiences there. The book, published in 1940, was entitled *Into the Darkness: Nazi Germany Today*. He met with many prominent members of the Reich. He was even able to watch their Hereditary Health Court or their racial hygiene proceedings that decided upon sterilization of the unfit. His description of Nazi Germany has many important ideas that provide insight into how these ideas linger within modern societies. Stoddard wrote:

> In Nazi eyes, the Gemeinschaft concept is best expressed by the word Volksgemeinschaft; literally, Folk Community. Note the difference between this and our idea of a nation. To us, a nation means the sum-total of all persons now living in the territory of a sovereign State who owe allegiance to it. The Nazi Folk or People differs from the traditional nation both in time and in space. Having a racial basis, its living members are links in a vital chain which includes both the dead and the unborn. Furthermore, all its blood-brothers are organically members, even though they live far from the political center of the Folk. Thus, persons of German blood throughout the world are presumed to have a sort of mystic tie with the Third Reich, no matter what their technical citizenship. On the other hand, resident Jews are not, and cannot become, full-fledged Reich citizens. They are merely Reich subjects. (Stoddard, 1940, p. 266)

Stoddard conveys a lot of information there about framing and nationality. First, nationality, or in this case, 'German' identity transcends borders. While he concedes Americans consider nationality differently, this statement also seems to be an attempt to link German-Americans into the greater sphere of the Reich and incorporate them as part of the larger whole. More importantly, the last two sentences highlight part of a rhetorical balancing act employed by Germany. Moreover, Donald Trump uses a similar framing in many of his speeches today. Stoddard separates the difference between citizens and subjects. Citizenship rights "rest on consent" (Kettner, 1978, p. 10) and "confer equal rights" (Kettner, 1978, p. 10). In other words, citizenship exists "as a right that can be officially chosen" (Brewer, 2007, p. 132), while subjects have "no choice over one's allegiance" (Brewer, 2007, p. 130). Subjects are governed, and citizens have greater rights within a society. Stoddard explains how Third Reich restrictions on persons of Jewish ancestry were acceptable because they lacked full standing within society, and as mere subjects, Germany could rule them as they saw fit. Citizenship by birthright was conveyed by ethnicity, not location. Jews born in Germany would never be able to attain the same citizenship status because they were not equal by birth. They were merely subjects expected to be ruled by the governing authority. Citizens and subjects are not synonymous. They are two different statuses within a society with very different rights and privileges.

Donald Trump says he wants to modify birthright citizenship. That is, children of non-citizens should not be given citizenship at birth. He seems to want to declare this group subjects with limited rights. This position contradicts the 14th Amendment, but the origins of these beliefs can be found in places like Lothrop Stoddard and Madison Grant's *The Passing of the Great Race* (1916). Grant was one of the icons of eugenic-based thought in the early twentieth century. This book was well regarded then, with sections read into the record during the 1924 immigration debates. Grant believed "universal suffrage tends towards the selection of the average man for public office rather than the man qualified by birth, education, and integrity" (Grant, 1916, p. 5). He believed "layer after layer of immigrants of lower races" (Grant, 1916, p. 5) weighs down the United States. In particular, the American sold his birthright in a continent to solve a labor problem. Instead of retaining political control and making citizenship an honorable and valued privilege, he intrusted the government of his country and the maintenances of his ideals to races who have never yet succeeded in governing themselves much less any one else. (Grant, 1916, p. 12)

Grant wanted to preserve the participation of those he considered worthy and make immigration more difficult to weed out those who did not fit his criteria.

Donald Trump, in the 2024 Presidential campaign, utilized racial and ethnic tropes to help galvanize his case. On January 8, 2024, Donald Trump, on TruthSocial, suggested that Nikki Haley was ineligible to run for president because her parents were not citizens at the time of her birth in 1972. She was born in South Carolina, and under the U.S. Constitution, she was granted citizenship at birth. The Fourteenth Amendment, Section 1, Clause 1 states, "All persons born or naturalized in the United States, and subjects to the jurisdiction thereof, are citizens of the United States and of the State wherein they reside" Her parents were not citizens at the time of her birth, and all standing law supports her citizenship. Trump has brought into question the validity of the idea of 'natural born.' He has previously rejected ideas of birthright citizenship, going as far as 2015 to claim that persons born to undocumented citizens in the United States are not granted citizenship at birth (Diamond, 2015). He has made similar statements after his administration ended (Hesson, 2023). He previously made extensive claims questioning the validity of Barack Obama's natural-born status, even though Obama's mother was born in Kansas. Since Barack Obama's mother's citizenship was never questioned, it should not have been given the level of attention it was as a presidential eligibility question (Barbaro, 2016). Haley's citizenship has never, and should never, be in question. Donald Trump has repetitively railed against 'anchor babies,' though he has stopped short of labeling Haley in such a way (Hillyard & Terkel, 2024). These positions embraced by Donald Trump strike at the heart of the subject versus citizen difference. Any rejection of birthright citizenship embraces the idea that persons born in the United States could perhaps only exist as subjects and not as total participants within the society. Subjects have limited rights, and it is acceptable to restrict their participation. On the other hand, citizenship suggests extended rights and few, if any, restrictions. Eugenicists see citizenship as something that should not be given lightly and restricted to the privileged few who see the world in similar ways as themselves.

IMMIGRANTS AND CONTROLLING BIRTH

Donald Trump's immigration policies and attitudes had long-ranging impacts. Many of these appear to be framed or impacted by eugenic perspectives. For most early twentieth-century adherents to eugenics, Northern Europeans of Anglo-Saxon (or Anglo-Teutonic) descent were considered humanity's intellectual and physical apex. Their ancestral heredity needed to be preserved or risk extinction. Marriage, sterilization, and immigration laws aimed at separation, segregation, containment, or isolation reflect desires to minimize potential interactions. Many Americans within the movement worried about the implications of American women seeking careers outside the home. Delays in motherhood meant fewer children, which would inevitably lend itself to losing ancestral dominance in America. Similar concerns surrounded the choice to have smaller families with fewer children, which they believed led to the same conclusion. (Iseman, 1912). These advocates were also staunchly anti-abortion because of the loss of White non-immigrant populations and not religious or moral grounds (Iseman, 1912; LeBeuf, 1904).

In many ways, Donald Trump is the inheritor of Theodore Roosevelt's attitudes about race suicide. Roosevelt was concerned over recent immigrant populations whose "alien habits which were not rapidly changed" (Dyer, 1980, p. 130) and "argued that Americanization primarily denoted the process of absorbing immigrants into the national bloodstream, the doctrine also referred to cultural assimilation and to Anglo-conformity" (Dyer, 1980, p. 133). Theodore Roosevelt hated hyphenation and "demanded that ethnics shed old ways" (Dyer, 1980, p. 133). However, for Roosevelt, assimilation was always tied to race. "Blacks, of course, did not qualify for assimilation and neither did Orientals or Latin Americans" (Dyer, 1980, p. 134). Roosevelt wanted America to be a melting pot with highly selective curated ingredients. His diversity lay within White immigrant ancestry, not racial integration.

> If Americans were to participate in world politics, they must realize that the 'competition between the races' has been reduced to the 'warfare of the cradle' and that no race had a change 'to win a great place' unless it consisted of 'good breeders as well as good fighters'. (Dyer, 1980, p. 145)

The real war, in other words, involves classes within the United States. Wealthier Americans who comprise 'old stock,' or long-standing families, are not expanding their populations as rapidly as those from more recent arrivals. Unless these groups change to grow their population, they will be supplanted within American society as the dominant force. In a letter, Roosevelt wrote, "our race ... is unfit to cumber the earth, if its men do not work hard ... and its women breed" (Dyer, 1980, pp. 148–149). Roosevelt believed a woman had an obligation to her race and to the United States to have a copious number of children. He denigrated women who chose to remain childless, equating them to soldiers who flee in the face of enemy fire (Dyer, 1980, p. 153). Roosevelt's views were stridently against birth control, termination, and decisions to remain childless. He linked patriotism to parenthood. During Roosevelt's sixth message to Congress in 1906, he requested "the whole question of marriage and divorce should be relegated to the authority of the National Congress" ("Sixth," 1906). He wanted the power to manage marriage and divorce at the national level, or more importantly, not divorce. Roosevelt wanted America to be a regulated but fertile utopia of White citizens. White women should aspire to produce large families, but simultaneously, Roosevelt did not extend that privilege to all. He embraced eugenic principles of selectivity, asserting "society could not permit 'degenerates to reproduce their kind' and found it 'really extraordinary that our people refuse to apply to a human being such elementary knowledge as ever farmer is obliged to apply to his own stock breeding'" (Dyer, 1980, p. 159). Theodore Roosevelt wanted America to have a large gene pool but also embraced sterilization of criminals and the feebleminded (Dyer, 1980, p. 161). He wanted eugenics professors to impress upon their students, which, at this time, meant White and male, that "it is their prime duty to their race to leave their seed after them to inherit the earth" (Dyer, 1980, p. 161). Roosevelt had a complicated relationship with eugenicists. He believed in their selectivity, yet simultaneously "placed considerable blame for the declining birthrate on eugenicists and on 'decadent' and 'immoral' birth control 'propagandists'" (Dyer, 1980, p. 164).

Donald Trump's position during his presidency suggested an affinity or appreciation for Roosevelt's beliefs. Donald Trump repetitively argued for restrictions on visas and immigration from places he felt were not worthy of citizenship. Simultaneously, he gave speeches embracing the rights of the unborn, thrilling pro-life advocates. With Trump's appointments to the Supreme Court, the *Dobbs v. Jackson Women's Health Organization* ruling unraveled the penumbra of nationalized rights to abortion access and devolved back down to a state-level regulation. Many people have written extensively in various forums about Trump's advocacy for issues salient to Christian conservatives. However, what if these groups are not as aligned as they are parallel? Trump's embrace of pro-life has less to do with the rights of fetuses but more to do with the control of population grown among specific populations within the United States. In 2023, Trump's message toward abortion politics slightly shifted, and he attempted to create a more moderating message (Lutz, 2023; Smith-Schoenwalder, 2024).

When filtered through a race-suicide lens, his positions on abortion make far greater sense. Donald Trump seems to want to restrict immigration heavily yet increase population totals. These two stances are only possible by impeding access to abortions. An article published in November 2023 (Dench et al., 2023) found that "fertility rates increased by 3, 3.8, and 4.7 percent for non-Hispanic white, non-Hispanic Black, and Hispanic women, respectively" (p. 12). Fertility rates also were tied to state access and travel times (McPhillips, 2023). These numbers do suggest abortion bans result in population increases. However, Donald Trump's position likely fits more into Roosevelt's view of the American population increases rather than an ethical concern over abortion (Kitchener et al., 2024). It is not about the morality of life but the propagation of the population. Terminations from women who are considered 'correct' Americans are abhorrent. They represent the loss of potential greatness within American society. In Roosevelt's time, this category was restricted mainly to Whites. While Donald Trump may hold some views consistent with it, many of his comments on this issue likely line up more closely by broadening it to those currently holding citizenship. In April 2024, Trump yet again modified his position on abortion, explicitly embracing a state-by-state approach and backing away from a national ban (Smith-Schoenwalder, 2024). This position has infuriated many conservative Republicans. Some advocate for more extensive national prohibitions, while others believe the issue will help galvanize Democratic voters in 2024 (Korecki & Edelman, 2024). The state-by-state approach appears to be internally consistent with older advocates of racial suicide who similarly gauged citizenship rights as flexible depending upon who they applied to at the time.

In the *Dobbs* concurrence, Justice Clarence Thomas calls for a reexamination of *Griswold v. Connecticut*, *Lawrence v. Texas*, and *Obergefell v. Hodges* (Beauchamp, 2022). He believes we must "correct the error" (Beauchamp, 2022) in the due process decision. Thomas asserts that unenumerated rights, or rights not stated explicitly in the Constitution, do not exist. His opinion harkens back to the language and rationales of persons like Theodore Roosevelt, who were at odds with certain factions within eugenics. Roosevelt wanted certain groups to flourish within American society, notably Whites. Eugenicists often advocated for birth control because they wanted to make sure every child was the best possible child. At times, these positions had things jointly in common, but at others, they dissented quite vigorously with each other. Birth control, universally applied, restricts a nation's natural birth rate and was considered an anathema to many persons who proselytized against race suicide. The *Griswold* ruling asserted that a couple has a right to privacy within a marriage.

Additionally, the choice of whether or not they choose to use birth control within that relationship falls under their marital privacy. The government or the physician does not have the right to restrict their access to birth control, and they have the right to decide the size of their family, not an outside third party. Thomas's call to reexamine this decision suggests he rejects the idea of marital privacy. If it does not exist as a fundamental right, the government could regulate it. In other words, the government could have the capacity to criminalize both birth control and abortion since privacy rights do not exist in the eyes of the government. These ideas gel with the language of an earlier era, which wanted to increase the 'best' stock of the country to make it as strong as possible.

IMMIGRANTS AND NON-AMERICAN POPULATIONS

In Minnesota, eugenics supporters openly asserted that "there was a hierarchy of races and worried about the potential dysgenic impact that immigration from Mexico and southern and eastern Europe would have on the United States" (Ladd-Taylor, 2017, p. 77). Donald Trump's regional biases have been prevalent throughout many comments toward countries, ethnicities, and other cultures. On June 16, 2015, Donald Trump delivered a speech declaring himself a presidential candidate. He connected concerns of immigration to crime in an incredibly abrasive tone, stating,

When Mexico sends its people, they're not sending their best. They're not sending you. They're not sending you. They're sending people that have lots of problems, and they're bringing those problems with us. They're bringing drugs. They're bringing crime. They're rapists. And some, I assume, are good people. ("Full Text," 2015)

When confronted by the statements in an interview with Don Lemon, Trump responded by saying, "'Well, somebody's doing the raping, Don! I mean somebody's doing it! Who's doing the raping? Who's doing the raping?' he asked" (Scott, 2015). His statements have similarities to the research conducted by Cesare Lombroso in the nineteenth century, who believed "certain biological types are predisposed ... by their heredity to commit crimes" (Weikart, 2004, p. 37). These ideas were rampant throughout many expert opinions on the subject, with "most other eugenicists used [using] the specter of the 'born criminal' or 'moral defective' to motivate their contemporaries to adopt eugenics policies" (Weikart, 2004, p. 41). Weikart (2004) points out that Felix van Luschan, a professor at the University of Berlin in the late nineteenth and early twentieth century, asserted, "Some crime is a hereditary disease, the way to solve the problem is by 'the complete and permanent isolation of the criminal'" (p. 41). By linking immigration, crime, and persons together in negative ways, Donald Trump projects well-established nativist tropes upon populations. These statements cast the group as the other and deserving of treatments that would not be acceptable to their own people. Much of this rhetoric has a more profound American eugenic influence. At the end of *Rising Tide of Color*, Lothrop Stoddard discusses how he feels the White race of America is under attack from immigration. "If the present drift is not changed, we whites are all ultimately doomed" (Stoddard, 1920, p. 304). He states, "We now know that men are not, and never will be equal. We now know that environment and education can only develop what heredity brings" (Stoddard, 1920, p. 306). In other words, non-White groups are genetically inferior, and no amount of intervention or socialization can change it. The only resource is heavily restricting immigration to prevent the loss of White hegemony and importance. For Stoddard, these ideas are not just speculation. His world was a zero-sum place where non-Whites consistently adhered to less-than-noble motivations to undermine his civilization into barbarism. The journal *American Medicine* in 1907 wrote, "editors of this professional journal ... among the many educated Americans who then accepted the brain weight and brain shape myths of scientific racism as scientific facts" (Chase, 1977, pp. 179–180). First,

> the brains of white people were larger, heavier, and structurally different from and mentally superior to those brains of Orientals, American Indians, Negroes, and other nonwhite people. ... physiological, mental and behavioral traits of every individual ... transmitted in the blood of all parents to their children. (Chase, 1977, p. 176)

These ideas persist in different iterations, often as euphemisms to frame arguments about the need to protect the United States, and especially White America, from other influences.

Donald Trump uses the term Mexican as a generalized negative ethnicity rather than a specific nationality. Furthermore, his usage reflected a generalized attitude toward Latin Americans, mainly Central Americans, rather than just one country. Donald Trump attacked Federal District Judge Gonzalo Curiel in June 2016 over his ancestral origins. He claimed a U.S. District Judge needed to be recused from a case concerning Trump University simply because he would be biased toward him for his ancestral background. "In an interview, Mr. Trump said U.S. District Judge Gonzalo Curiel had 'an absolute conflict' in presiding over the litigation given that he was 'of Mexican heritage' and a member of a Latino lawyers' association" (Kendall, 2016; Kertscher, 2016). Trump said in an interview, "'I have a Mexican judge. He's of Mexican heritage. He should have recused himself, not only for that, for other things' even though the cases were not related" (Rappeport, 2016). Donald Trump conflates race and professionalism as indistinguishable from each other. He also claimed that because of the judge's Mexican ancestral origins, "it's an inherent conflict of interest" (Ford, 2016) even though he was born in the United States.

During a May 2018 meeting about undocumented immigrants in California, President Trump said, "You wouldn't believe how bad these people are. These aren't people, these are animals, and we're taking them out of the country at a level and at a rate that's never happened before" (Davis, 2018). In June 2017, President Trump complained that all recent Haitian immigrants have AIDS and Nigerians "would never 'go back to their huts' once they saw America" (Marcin, 2017; Shear & Davis, 2017). While the White House did not dispute the overall comment but did claim the president did not use the words AIDS or huts, though reports appear to contradict it. These beliefs seemed consistent throughout the Trump administration. In May 2019, when he was giving a speech in Panama City, Florida, about stopping migrants at the border, there was an exchange where someone in the audience shouted, 'Shoot them.' Trump paused and smirked before responding, "That's only in the Panhandle can you get away with that statement" (Rieger, 2019).

During his third presidential run in 2024, Donald Trump continued negative portrayals of immigrants. On March 4, 2024, he said that migrants

> 'They're rough people, in many cases from jails, prisons, from mental institutions, insane asylums' continuing saying 'You know, insane asylums, that's 'Silence of the Lambs' stuff.' He went on to ask if people knew of Hannibal Lecter and 'We don't want 'em in this country'. (Lebowitz & Traylor, 2024)

He has repetitively compared immigrants to the cannibal serial killer in the 1988 Thomas Harris novel and 1991 movie. In the same March 4 interview, Trump compared foreign languages to Mars. "'We don't even have teachers of some of these languages. Who would think that? We have languages that are, like, from, from the planet Mars?' Trump said. 'Nobody, nobody knows how to, you know, speak it'" (Lebowitz & Traylor, 2024). On March 16, 2024, Trump further framed immigrants in dehumanizing ways, stating, "'These are bad — these are animals,' he added. 'And we have to stop it'" (Wade, 2024). Many of these talking points Donald Trump uses, both as a candidate and president, echo similar concerns about the restrictions put in place leading up to and during the passage of the Immigration Act of 1924. The underlying theme then and now with Donald Trump revolves around the idea that racially diverse individuals are weakening the fortitude of the nation. Their blood weakens ours. For eugenicists, it always comes down to blood and genetic heritage. Genius, deficiency, and inheritance all originate in our blood. We weaken ourselves and our birthright when we allow others into our society. Madison Grant wrote, "the American sold his birthright to solve a labor problem" (Grant, 1916, p. 12).

In a December 2023 speech, Donald Trump said, "They're poisoning the blood of our country" (Fischler, 2023) to supporters in Durham, New Hampshire, referring to immigrants. He continued with,

That's what they've done. They've poisoned mental institutions and prisons all over the world, not just in South America, not just the three or four countries that we think about, but all over the world. They're coming into our country, from Africa, from Asia, all over the world. Nobody's even looking at it". (Fischler, 2023)

During a November 2023 speech, Donald Trump stated that his political opponents within the United States were 'vermin' and a "greater threat to the United States than countries such as Russia, China or North Korea" (LeVine, 2023). Trump's language toward his political enemies and immigrants drew criticism, with some calling parallels to Adolf Hitler's book, *Mein Kampf*. Donald Trump responded by saying, "'I never read 'Mein Kampf,' Trump said at a campaign rally in Waterloo, Iowa, referencing Adolf Hitler's fascist manifesto" (Fingerhut & Swenson, 2023). Donald Trump may have never read *Mein Kampf*, but his language evokes American eugenicists in very close ways. Harry H. Laughlin, in his testimony in front of the Committee on Immigration and Naturalization in the House of Representatives on April 17, 1920, spoke about the need for immigration regulations. "The character of our future civilization will be modified by the 'blood' or the national hereditary qualities which the sexually fertile immigrant brings to our shores" (Laughlin, 1920, p. 8). Laughlin testifies, "Our failure to sort immigrants on the basis of national worth is a very serious national menace" (Laughlin, 1920, p. 17). His testimony centers around the idea that a significant number of aliens on American soil drain our resources through incarceration in mental institutions, hospitals, and elsewhere. While many people were quick to point out similarities to *Mein Kampf*, deeper roots are at play. This rhetoric has long been associated with eugenicists in the United States. Ordover (2003) points out that "eugenicists constantly lamented the 'watering down of our nation's life-blood' by the admission and procreation of 'alien defectives'" (p. 7). Balibar and Wallerstein (1991) says, "racism first presents itself as a super-nationalism. ... Racism sees itself as an 'integral nationalism which only has meaning (and changes of success) if it is based on the integrity of the nation...'" (p. 59). Although dense, Balibar & Wallerstein's words read prophetic toward the emergence of American populism in the twenty-first century. They state, "racism always tends to operate in an inverted fashion, drawing upon the projection mechanism ... the racial-cultural identity of the 'true nationals' remains invisible, but it can be inferred (and is ensured) *a contrario* by the alleged quasi-hallucinatory visibility of the 'false nationals'" (Balibar & Wallerstein, 1991, p. 60).

Donald Trump appears to have long-held views that fall very consistent with the historical perspectives of racial suicide and eugenics. He has built his campaign platforms on illegal immigration framed around the idea that these immigrants are "destroying the blood of our country, they're destroying the fabric of our country" (Gold, 2023). He has still engaged in dehumanizing language to cast people in objective ways. "In some cases they're not people, in my opinion" (Leingang, 2024). There have been other Trump administration policies that seem to reinforce segregationist ethnicity strategies. In particular, the policies of travel bans for people from Muslim-dominated countries (Kanno-Youngs, 2020), zero tolerance for undocumented persons and child separation at the border (Horwitz & Sacchetti, 2018), restrictions on asylum (Liptak, 2021), and attempts to end H-1B visas (Anderson, 2021) all suggest the Trump administration wanted to pursue policies that would allow the United States to differentiate between certain ancestral, racial, or ethnic groups. Gamboa (2020) noted the administration's call "for a show of hands among senior officials on separating children from parents is being called 'a damning display of white supremacy.'"

Donald Trump, as a candidate and president, gave speeches with views adversarial toward Muslims. He indicated support for a Muslim registry in the United States. When asked about what the "difference is between a registry for Muslims and the registry for Jews under Nazi Germany, to which Trump only replied, 'You tell me'" (Carroll, 2015). Though Trump later claimed the reporter was the only one who mentioned a registry, he later clarified his words, saying, "what I want is a watch list. I want surveillance programs" (Carroll, 2015). In 2016 after bombings tied to Muslims in French and Belgian Muslims in Brussels, Donald Trump "called for surveillance of mosques in the United States, saying: 'You have to deal with the mosques, whether we like it or not, I mean, you know, these attacks aren't coming out of – they're not done by Swedish people" (Johnson & Hauslohner, 2017). These comments echo similar Nordicism language routinely used by Donald Trump regarding different ethnic populations. During campaigning in 2023, he read a poem on campaign stops "to liken immigrants to deadly snakes" (Layne & Reid, 2023). He has also pledged to "bring back a travel ban 'even bigger than before,' alluding to his administration's restrictions on travelers from heavily Muslim countries" (Watson & Hudak, 2023).

Throughout the entire Trump administration, they attempted to curtail H-1B visas. "While Donald Trump often said he wanted 'merit-based' immigration, the war against companies, international students, and H-1B visa holders during his administration showed the president and this appointed team had little interest in admitting even the most highly skilled foreign nationals to America" (Anderson, 2021). These visas admit "foreign professionals to work in 'specialty occupations' that require at least a bachelor's degree or the equivalent. Jobs in fields such as mathematics, engineering, technology, and medical sciences often qualify" ("The H1-B," 2021). During the fiscal year 2018, 73.9% of all H-1B petitions were from India, and 11.2% were citizens of the People's Republic of China ("H-1B Petitions," 2018). After these two nationalities, the remaining countries fall in the one percent or lower range for applicants.

Race, ancestry, and immigration all intertwine into the same universe. Lothrop Stoddard had tremendous influence over racial attitudes in the 1920s and continues today. He perceived Whites as the only ones capable of orderly civilization (Stoddard, 1920, p. 8), but other groups reproduced faster. Stoddard referred to Latin America in *Rising Tide* as the Red Man's Land and struggled with his categorizations. He felt that White colonial influences there were strong but undermined by co-mingling with other groups. Stoddard believed the only places that developed stable governments, like Chile, created them through White oligarchical structures (Stoddard, 1920, pp. 110–111). He claimed that marriage between Whites and non-Whites undermined these societies. Specifically, he asserted that predominantly White settled Costa Rica was the only one that "rises an oasis of civilization, above the tropic jungle of degenerate, mongrel Central America" (Stoddard, 1920, p. 113). In 1944, Ira Calvin wrote *The Lost White Race*, where he argued for segregation in the United States but asserted the only real solution lay within physical separation. "The setting up and establishment of a separate State for the Negro is the only way in which can save him, and at the same time not drown ourselves in the process" (Calvin, 1944, p. 181). Calvin argues for a "buffer State between us and Mexico" (Calvin, 1944, p. 177) to remove Blacks from America physically. His rhetoric and language sound familiar to things echoed 70 years later by Donald Trump arguing for a wall of separation. Calvin says, "the one thing that makes it imperative that we lose no time in establishing a State for the Negro is the great increase in the rape and murder of white girls by Negro men" (Calvin, 1944, p. 178). These assertions are presented without any evidence but just as anecdotes. He points out these separations are not altruistic. Specifically, Calvin is worried about diminishing electoral power, stating, "for the way they multiply because of the widespread knowledge of birth-control, maybe in a few hundred years they would outnumber us, outvote us, and even exterminate us" (Calvin, 1944, p. 177). When looking at Donald Trump's language toward Blacks, immigration, immigrants, and election fraud, there seems to exist far stronger links to Ira Calvin's writings than to Adolf Hitler. In a February 2024 speech, Trump said, "'Welcome to the Congo, people,' he said, claiming Africans were coming from prisons and asylums. He promised 'the largest deportation in history'" (Calmes, 2024) with language very feels reminiscent of these early twentieth-century eugenicists.

Trump and His Use of Mocking and Slurs

There have been numerous other instances of Donald Trump using race or racial allusions toward individuals to mock them (Cineas, 2021; Graham et al., 2019; Lopez, 2020). Trump repeatedly frames things in a racial, ancestral, or 'fit' lens to justify or support his positions. Donald Trump once referred to a Latina woman crowned Miss Universe as 'Miss Housekeeping' and 'Miss Piggy' ("Alicia Machado," 2016). When confronted about it during his 2016 presidential run, Trump did not refute the comments and instead stood by them, claiming she was not a good Miss Universe (Gonzalez, 2016). He ridiculed the physical disability of a reporter during a 2015 campaign speech (Mackey, 2017). In March 2024, Trump started mocking Joe Biden for his stutter (Gold, 2024b). During a March 10, 2024, speech in Rome, Georgia, he criticized President Biden's recent State of the Union address, mocking it and specifically said, 'Bring the country t-t-t-t-together' to highlight Biden's disability (Aster, 2024). He has repeatedly mocked people for their weight (Vazquez, 2019; Zezima & DelReal, 2016). After Donald Trump was indicted in Georgia over the election results, he posted that they should have tried to find the people who rigged the election. Specifically, he wrote, "They only went after those that fought to find the RIGGERS!" which his former aide, Alyssa Farah Griffith, referred to as a dog whistle, or thinly veiled racial slur (Harvey, 2023).

4 DONALD TRUMP'S RHETORIC AND HOW EUGENICS ... 95

What Is the Purpose of a Slur?

The determination of a slur relies upon whether "they possess a common capacity [within] a slurring word to dehumanize" (Jeshion, 2013, p. 232). Jeshion (2013) provides five categories for evaluating a statement. First, do they "function to signal that their targets are unworthy of equal standing or full respect as persons" (p. 232)? Next, it aims to "derogate in the same way" ... and "same degree," and also "the power of the words themselves" (Jeshion, 2013, p. 232). Most important, Donald Trump's language rests with the fourth point: the "slurs' capacity to derogate is closely associated with the speaker's intent to do so" (Jeshion, 2013, p. 232). In September 2022, Donald Trump referred to New York Attorney General Letitia James as "Racist A.G. Letitia 'Peekaboo' James" (Norton, 2022). Peekaboo is exceptionally similar to two different terms historically used as insults toward Black persons.

Donald Trump's statement about Letitia James falls into the category of a slur regardless of the racial history of the words or partial words used toward her. He assigned a nickname with strong alliteration from archaic, demeaning American slang. It implies an intent to assign inferiority to the words without requiring a Rosetta Stone to break the thinly coded language. Consequently, it checks every Jeshion's criteria to qualify as a slur. While uncomfortable, the origins of words often belie their meanings. Donald Trump's usage of peekaboo likely involves a mashup of the terms 'jigaboo' and 'pickaninny.' The latter is more straightforward to decipher because it has roots in a Portuguese word for a small child. It has been used since the 1800s to often refer to dark-skinned children in many countries (Bernstein, 2011). Jigaboo has a more complex history. In 1909, there was a play called 'The Midnight Sons.' In this play, an Irishman, Jim O'Shea, is cast away on an island near India. He was called 'Jij-ji-boo' which morphed into the other term. There was a popular song in the play called 'I've Got Rings on My Fingers.' It was often sung in minstrel performances by White performers wearing dark makeup. The wide popularity of it helped launch the term into more common usage, becoming part of derogatory vernacular toward persons of color (Brown, 2022; "Dover Women," 1909).

This incident is not the only time in recent memory that Donald Trump has used words to make thinly veiled race-based insults. He seems to target women more frequently with this specific type of charged language. Nikki Haley was Nimarata Nikki Randhawa at birth, though she has always used the nickname Nikki, a familiar term for a child. In January 2024, Donald Trump began mocking her first name by calling her 'Nimbra' and 'Nimrada' (Barrow, 2024; Blake, 2024). Both are intentional mispronunciations of her first name. These are apparent attempts to amp up references to her Indian Sikh heritage. All Asians, including ones from the Indian subcontinent, were barred from immigration after the Immigration Act of 1917. This law was the forerunner of the 1924 act, which imposed far more sweeping restrictions. The law existed until the Immigration and Nationality Act of 1952, which removed the blanket ban on all Asians. Trump's mispronunciations attempt to slur and demean. The latter nickname likely involves Trump trying to make it sound similar to the English word, 'nimrod,' which is historically used as a slight toward a person who is inept or foolish. The word became popular when Warner Bros. used it in 1948 and 1951 toward Elmer Fudd and then Yosemite Sam in derogatory ways (Zurski, 2021). Intentionally mispronouncing names is a low-level aggressive way to insult a person and "is a form of casual racism that promotes the superiority of white people and western ideals" (Elkharssa, 2021). Donald Trump repetitively uses nicknames as a way to mock others but most frequently uses racially charged language toward women. During an April 2024 speech, Trump mocked and engaged in derogatory comments about Fani Willis's name. He also imposed his own opinions on her name. "It's spelled fanny like your ass, right? Fanny. But when she became DA, she decided to add a little French, a little fancy" (Leingang, 2024). There is a Wikipedia list where they compile terms Donald Trump has used toward others. As of April 2024, there were 75 different people, groups, or organizations in which he has used or applied insulting names. Most of these names employ an adjective before their first or last name, with a negative and often alliterative connotation. Within this list, only women of color receive terms that are racial pejoratives ("List of," 2024). Women of color are referred to as 'Coco Chow' (Elaine Chow), 'Peekaboo' (Letitia James), 'Evita' (Alexandria Ocasio-Cortez), 'Pocahontas' (Elizabeth Warren), 'Low-IQ Maxine Waters' (Maxine Waters), 'Nimrada/ Nimbra' (Nikki Haley), 'That dog' (Omarosa Manigault Newman) and 'Phoney Fani' (Fani Willis). These racially charged terms are distinctive from other insults he uses toward White women: 'Crazy Liz Cheney' (Liz Cheney), 'Crazy/Crooked/Lyin' Hillary' (Hillary Clinton), 'Disaster from Alaska' (Lisa Murkowski), 'Crazy/Nervous Nancy' (Nancy

Pelosi), 'Wacky Jacky' (Jacky Rosen), and 'That woman from Michigan' (Gretchen Whitmer) (Table 4.1).

Insults toward men more closely resemble those assigned to White women, and there exists a clear racial distinction in the level of personalized ethically charged insults toward non-White women. It suggests a

Table 4.1 Nicknames Donald Trump assigned to Americans as of April 2024

White men	White women	Men of color	Women of color
Aida	Beautiful	Lyin'	Birdbrain
Alfred E. Newman	Crazy	Little	Coco Chow
Basement	Crooked		Evita
Beijing	Disaster from Alaska		Nimrada
Birdbrain	Ditzy		Nimbra
Boot-Edge-Edge	Goofy		Peekaboo
Broken Old Crow	Lyin'		Tricky-Nikki
Crazy	Nervous		Pocohontas (Elizabeth Warren)
Cryin'	Pocohontas (Elizabeth Warren)		Wacky
Deranged	Wacky		
DeSanctimonious			
Flakey			
Leakin'			
Liddle'			
Little			
Low Energy			
Mad Dog			
McMuffin			
Mini			
Moonbeam			
My			
Newscum			
Pencil Neck			
Rob			
Rob DeSanctimonious			
RINO			
Shady			
Sleepy			
Sloppy			
Slow			
Tiny-D			
Wild			

clear pattern of targeted humiliation that frames itself around targeting their non-Whiteness as a cause for his ire. Terms matter because they suggest how Donald Trump frames the target within his rhetoric. Women of color are frequently assigned terms that objectify them in terms of an ethnic or racial characteristic. The word evokes another person vaguely associated with that term or functions as a veiled alliteration or allusion to another word that is frequently unacceptable or moderately profane, referencing racial or ethnic aspects. Their entire person flattens into a racially defined space. When Donald Trump assigns nicknames to others, they are almost always in the realm of character traits. He assigns nicknames based on attributes he wants to associate with them. He wants to paint targets as liars, inept, or usually some negative connotation.

Donald Trump, Fit, Health, and Religion

For advocates of eugenics, superiority is conveyed via fitness and health. Good genes promote both vitality and vigor. Donald Trump's need to be perceived as healthy and fit falls in line with the attitudes of the Eugenics Movement. Public health was long a concern of the movement (Pernick, 1997), and the Muscular Christianity movement thrived upon the ideas promoting the "body as temple… many came perilously close to calling musclemen saints and the sick sinners" (Putney, 2001, p. 57). Good health and fitness were idolized as indicators of superior genes, while any weaknesses betrayed inferiorities. During his presidential run, Trump's physician released a letter claiming he "will be the healthiest individual ever elected to the presidency" (Brait, 2015). This is a specious claim given the lack of thorough medical documentation on most previous presidents. Three years later, it was revealed that this medical report was written by Donald Trump and merely signed by a physician (McCarthy, 2018). In other words, Donald Trump entirely made up a health report to intentionally craft a false narrative. Throughout his presidency, Donald Trump had doctors regularly claim his health was 'good' (Smith, 2018). In 2018, the White House physician, when discussing Trump's health, said, "'It's called genetics,' Dr. Jackson said of the president's good health. 'I told the president if he had eaten healthier over the last 20 years, he might live to be 200'" (Karni & Altman, 2019).

In October 2020, President Trump tested positive for COVID-19. He was treated and placed on experimental protocols, given his severe symptoms (Morales et al., 2020; O'Donnell, 2020). Within days of contracting the virus, he left the hospital and downplayed its impact on him (Baker & Haberman, 2020). There were concerns at the time about his contagiousness that the White House dismissed. They minimized any reports, even when his disclosed treatments were only for the most severe cases. A few months later, it was revealed he was extremely ill, almost placed on a ventilator, and likely left the hospital too early (Weiland et al., 2021). His decision to downplay his medical issues and present an image of invulnerability meshes well with the general worldview of eugenics. Health is tied to vigor and overall physical superiority. Illness betrays weakness and suggests you are not the best or most fit. Trump could not be ill because his narrative of vitality could not be compromised. The illusion of his physical superiority had to be maintained. As scholars and citizens, we observe these events, judge them for their outrageousness, and seem surprised by their lack of impact upon his most fervent supporters. Historical eugenic undertones are so engrained within the fabric of certain aspects of American society that they are overlooked. Generations of nineteenth and twentieth-century White Americans were taught about their inherent superiority in schools and Protestant religious life. They were indoctrinated into popular culture through books, plays, and movies (Leung, 2014). These lessons were not immediately jettisoned with the Nuremberg trials at the end of the Second World War. America quietly removed much of the overt material from classrooms, but values often persist through conversation and social attitudes.

While aspects faded, particular worldviews stubbornly persisted and continued. In the 2016 and 2020 elections, 50% of mainline Protestants supported Donald Trump (Burge, 2021). However, those numbers move to 78% and 80% when looking at White evangelicals (Burge, 2021). The White evangelical support is notable because of their overwhelming approval. On the other hand, Black Protestants backed Trump in 2016 at 7% and in 2020 at 9%. These broad differences are striking and suggest there is more afoot than religiosity. Race would not create such a stark contrast if it were solely Protestantism as a driving factor.

Donald Trump complained about the lack of support among other religious groups in a September 2021 phone call with faith leaders. Specifically, he complained about "losing votes from ungrateful Catholics and Jews in the 2020 election" (Papenfuss, 2021). In 2020, Trump won 59% of the White Catholic vote (up from 57%) and 30% of the non-White Catholic vote (up from 26%) (Burge, 2021). Regarding Jewish voters, Trump carried 29% of the vote (up from 27%) (Burge, 2021). In other words, while Trump gained ground with both groups, it was minimal. He pursued policies and goals catering to their bases but did not see a direct electoral payoff. They highlight that Donald Trump views much of the United States in the New Deal Coalition delineations that dominated politics during the mid-twentieth century.

However, many of these groups have been fractured or reduced in importance as other social alignments have supplanted them. Many people no longer consider themselves primarily Catholic or Jewish, but rather, it is simply another component of themselves within a kaleidoscope of other descriptors. Donald Trump, however, apparently still sees them as monolithic groups that owe loyalty for favors. During this interview, Trump discussed his lack of support with the Jewish community. "Look what I did with the embassy in Jerusalem and what I did with so many other things ... Israel has never had a better friend, and yet I got 25% of the vote,' said Trump. 'I think they have to get together'" (Papenfuss, 2021). In Trump's worldview, people are simplistic categories and should be predictable in those ways. In 2019, Donald Trump stated that "Jews who vote for Democrats as 'very disloyal' to Israel" (Smith, 2019). In a June 2021 interview, he noted, "Jewish people who live in the United States don't love Israel enough" (Turx, 2021). In October 2022, Trump said Jews in the United States must "get their act together" and show more appreciation for the state of Israel "before it is too late" (Helderman, 2022). He maintained that stance even in March 2024, saying "'Any Jewish person that votes for Democrats hates their religion' and they 'should be ashamed of themselves'" (Lebowitz, 2024). He continued in April 2024, stating "any Jewish person that votes for Biden does not love Israel, and frankly, should be spoken to" (Gold, 2024b). These continued remarks toward Americans of Jewish faith strongly insinuate Donald Trump sees people categorized by race, ethnicity, or religion more than nationality. From this perspective, American Jews must place their faith above their country and, in doing so, set the nation of Israel paramount. He thus believes since he exhibited a solid partnership with Israel, American Jews should be loyal to him by default. Trump has displayed frustration this perspective has not been realized, posting a meme on TruthSocial toward the end of Rosh Hashana in 2023, "excoriating 'liberal Jews' who had 'voted to destroy America' with the caption saying 'Let's hope you learned from your mistake and make better choices going forward!'" (Rosenberg, 2023). These viewpoints also harken back to concepts of citizen and subject. Subjects are ruled and do as told within a society. Donald Trump's persistent and repetitive expectations that Americans of Jewish faith personally owe him for supporting another country raises serious questions about how he indeed views their citizenship rights within the United States.

Donald Trump's perspective toward Jewish people feels starkly reminiscent of the prevalent attitudes in the 1920s toward persons of the Catholic faith. Presidential candidate Al Smith was viciously attacked in 1928. He was criticized for his religious Catholic beliefs, and Protestant detractors stoked fears over whether he would be loyal to the United States or the Vatican. These loyalty tropes were recycled again in the 1960 campaign with John F. Kennedy, who ardently campaigned and won the West Virginia primary to help silence critics over his national viability at the top of the presidential ticket. Donald Trump sees the world in stark ethnic-religious terms when applied outside himself. He has recent German and Scottish ancestry, but no one questions his national loyalty. He finds it acceptable, however, to assume all Jewish Americans, regardless of the length of their generational ties to the United States, hold stronger loyalty to a country younger than himself.

Conclusion

The American Eugenics Movement was a period of history frequently swept under the rug and politely ignored. We try to dismiss eugenics as a distasteful foreign concept tied to the Nazis and Holocaust. By treating it this way, America sidesteps and overlooks its culpability and responsibilities to the past and present. These beliefs were widely accepted. They were not a fringe movement. Eugenics explicitly shaped laws and policies for about a half-century. When it fell from favor, the ideas became more understated but did not disappear. Donald Trump and much of his administration behaved as the embodiment of many of their ideals and beliefs. Trump seems to embrace a worldview sculpted by eugenic ideas that promote concepts of genetic superiority, especially among descendants with predominantly Anglo-Saxon ancestry. They allow adherents to justify discriminatory policies as fair because they protect an inherent hierarchy among those they perceive as more civilized. Others are often objectified or caricatured to dismiss any challenges. Immigration, especially from anywhere outside of Northwestern Europe, upsets America's immigration purity. Groups outside these narrow ethnicities must be contained or curtailed to fend off racial dilution. Eugenic perspectives promote a 'manifest destiny'-like mindset for the fate of the United States. America belongs to the White Protestants, and encroachments upon this dominance must be dealt with decisively.

Uncomfortable moments in our country's history should not be ignored because they are distasteful. We must tackle these periods, excise their findings, and place them within a proper context while fostering contemporary discussions of the works. When we are silent, many assume acceptance toward agendas embracing now obscure concepts and ideas. We cannot change the past, but we can become its stewards. History is only repeated when we do not carefully examine and learn from it.

References

Alicia Machado: Ex-Miss Universe Claims Trump Called Her 'Miss Piggy.' (2016, September 27). *BBC News*. https://www.bbc.com/news/world-us-canada-37488060

Anderson, S. (2021, February 1). The Story of How Trump Officials Tried to End H-1B Visas. *Forbes*. https://www.forbes.com/sites/stuartanderson/2021/02/01/the-story-of-how-trump-officials-tried-to-end-h-1b-visas/?sh=7f2fcfe1173f

Aster, M. (2024, March 11). Trump's Biden Mockery Upsets People Who Stutter: 'We've Heard This Before.' *The New York Times*. https://www.nytimes.com/2024/03/11/us/politics/trump-mocks-biden-stutter.html

Ayers, O. (2021). Fred Trump, the Klu Klux Klan and Grassroots Redlining in Interwar America. *Journal of Urban History, 47*(1), 3–28.

Baker, P., & Haberman, M. (2020, October 5). Trump Leaves Hospital, Minimizing Virus and Urging Americans 'Don't Let It Dominate Your Lives.' *The New York Times*. https://www.nytimes.com/2020/10/05/us/politics/trump-leaves-hospital-coronavirus.html

Balibar, E., & Wallerstein, I. (1991). *Race, Nation, Class: Ambiguous Identities*. Verso.

Barbaro, M. (2016, September 16). Donald Trump Cling to 'Birther' Lie for Years, and Still Isn't Apologetic. *The New York Times*. https://www.nytimes.com/2016/09/17/us/politics/donald-trump-obama-birther.html

Barnett, W. (1979, January 15). How a Young Donald Trump Forced His Way from Avenue Z to Manhattan. *The Village Voice*. https://www.villagevoice.com/2015/07/20/how-a-young-donald-trump-forced-his-way-from-avenue-z-to-manhattan/

Barrow, B. (2024, January 20). Trump Mocks Nikki Haley's First Name. It's His Latest Example of Attacking Rivals Based on Race. *Associated Press*. https://apnews.com/article/trump-nikki-haley-58b7ffa7e49f626bae481060cf9975d2

Beauchamp, Z. (2022, June 24). Could Clarence Thomas's Dobbs Concurrence Signal a Future Attack on LGBTQ Rights? *Vox*. https://www.vox.com/2022/6/24/23181723/roe-v-wade-dobbs-clarence-thomas-concurrence

Bernstein, R. (2011). *Racial Innocence*. New York University Press.

Blake, A. (2024, January 17). Trump Unsubtle Crusade to Cast Foes as Less American Comes for Haley. *The Washington Post*. https://www.washingtonpost.com/politics/2024/01/17/trump-playbook-foes-haley/

Brait, E. (2015, December 14). Donald Trump Would Be America's Healthiest President, Doctor's Letter Says. *The Guardian*. https://www.theguardian.com/us-news/2015/dec/14/donald-trump-health-doctor-letter-americas-healthiest-president

Brewer, H. (2007). *By Birth of Consent: Children, Law, and the Anglo-American Revolution in Authority*. The University of North Carolina Press.

Brockell, G. (2023, April 4). Donald Trump's Father Was Arrested, Too. *The Washington Post*. https://www.washingtonpost.com/history/2023/04/04/fred-trump-arrests/

Brown, P. J. (2022, March 22). 'Ji-ji-boo J. O'Shea'-How the Name of a Stranded Irishman Became a Pejorative Term for Black People. *Early Sports and Pop Culture History Blog*. https://esnpc.blogspot.com/2022/03/ji-ji-boo-j-oshea-how-name-of-stranded.html

Burge, R. (2021, April 8). Faith in Numbers: Trump Held Steady among Believers at the Ballot—It Was the Nonreligious Vote He Lost in 2020. *The Conversation*. https://theconversation.com/faith-in-numbers-trump-held-steady-among-believers-at-the-ballot-it-was-the-nonreligious-vote-he-lost-in-2020-158513

Calmes, J. (2024, February 22). Calmes: I Watched a Trump Rally so You Don't Have to. But You Need to Know What He's Saying. *Los Angeles Times*. https://www.yahoo.com/news/calmes-watched-trump-rally-dont-110253003.html

Calvin, I. (1944). *The Lost White Race*. Countway-White Publications.

Carian, E. K., & Sobotka, T. C. (2018). Playing the Trump Card: Masculinity Threat and the U.S. 2016 Presidential Election. *Socius*, *4*. https://doi.org/10.1177/2378023117740699

Carroll, L. (2015, November 24). In Context: Donald Trump's Comments on a Database of American Muslims. *Politifact*. https://www.politifact.com/article/2015/nov/24/donald-trumps-comments-database-american-muslims/

Chait, J. (2020, October 11). Trump's Lifelong Obsession with His Superior DNA Is Being Put to the Test. *New York*. https://nymag.com/intelligencer/2020/10/donald-trump-genetic-delusions-and-covid-19.html

Chase, A. (1977). *The Legacy of Malthus: The Social Costs of the New Scientific Racism*. Random House.

Cineas, F. (2021, January 9). Donald Trump Is the Accelerant. *Vox*. https://www.vox.com/21506029/trump-violence-tweets-racist-hate-speech

Cohen, A. S. (2016, March–April). Harvard's Eugenics Era. *Harvard Magazine*. https://www.harvardmagazine.com/2016/03/harvards-eugenics-era

Cox, E. S. (1923). *White America*. White America Society.

Cox, E. S. (1925). *White America* (Revised ed.). White America Society.

Davis, J. H. (2018, May 16). Trump Calls Some Unauthorized Immigrants 'Animals' in Rant. *The New York Times*. https://www.nytimes.com/2018/05/16/us/politics/trump-undocumented-immigrants-animals.html

Dawsey, J. (2018, January 12). Trump Derides Protections for Immigrants from 'Shithole' Countries. *The Washington Post*. https://www.washingtonpost.com/politics/trump-attacks-protections-for-immigrants-from-shithole-countries-in-oval-office-meeting/2018/01/11/bfc0725c-f711-11e7-91af-31ac729add94_story.html

Dench, D., Pineda-Torres, M., & Myers, C. (2023, November). The Effects of the Dobbs Decision on Fertility. *IZA Institute of Labor Economics*. https://docs.iza.org/dp16608.pdf

Diamond, J. (2015, August 19). Donald Trump: Birthright Babies Not Citizens. *CNN*. https://www.cnn.com/2015/08/19/politics/donald-trump-birthright-american-citizenship/index.html

Dover Women as Minstrels. (1909, November 11). *The Morning News*, p. 2.

Dyer, T. G. (1980). *Theodore Roosevelt and the Idea of Race*. Louisiana State University Press.

Elkharssa, Y. (2021, November 3). Put Some Respect On My Name. *The Michigan Daily*. https://www.michigandaily.com/michigan-in-color/put-some-respect-on-my-name/

Fingerhut, H., & Swenson, A. (2023, December 19). Trump Defends Controversial Comments About Immigrants Poisoning the Nation's Blood at Iwa Rally. *Associated Press*. https://apnews.com/article/donald-trump-immigration-iowa-dff7f632948fa6511fb7d1955a28610c

Fischler, J. (2023, December 18). Trump Borrows from the Language of Hitler for Anti-immigration Speech in New Hampshire. *Missouri Independent*. https://missouriindependent.com/2023/12/18/trump-borrows-from-the-language-of-hitler-for-anti-immigration-speech-in-new-hampshire/

Ford, M. (2016, June 3). Why Is Donald Trump so Angry at Judge Gonzalo Curiel? *The Atlantic*. https://www.theatlantic.com/politics/archive/2016/06/donald-trump-gonzalo-curiel/485636/

Full Text: Donald Trump Announces a Presidential Bid. (2015, June 16). *The Washington Post.* https://www.washingtonpost.com/news/post-politics/wp/2015/06/16/full-text-donald-trump-announces-a-presidential-bid/

Gamboa, S. (2020, August 22). 'White Supremacy' Was Behind Child Separations-and Trump Officials Went Along, Critics Say. *NBC News.* https://www.nbcnews.com/news/latino/white-supremacy-was-behind-child-separations-trump-officials-went-along-n1237746

Gold, M. (2023, December 22). Trump's Long Fascination with Genes and Bloodlines Gets New Scrutiny. *The New York Times.* https://www.nytimes.com/2023/12/22/us/politics/trump-blood-comments.html

Gold, M. (2024a, April 10). Trump Again Insults Jews Who Support Biden. *The New York Times.* https://www.nytimes.com/2024/04/10/us/politics/trump-jews-biden.html

Gold, M. (2024b, March 10). Trump Vilifies Migrants and Mocks Biden's Stutter in Georgia Speech. *The New York Times.* https://www.nytimes.com/2024/03/10/us/politics/trump-biden-georgia-rally.html

Gonzalez, D. (2016, September 27). Donald Trump Doubles Down on Comments About Latina Former Miss Universe. *AZCentral.* https://www.azcentral.com/story/news/politics/elections/2016/09/27/donald-trump-doubles-down-comments-former-miss-universe/91177530/

Graham, D. A., Green, A., Murphy, C., & Richards, P. (2019, June). An Oral History of Trump's Bigotry. *The Atlantic.* https://www.theatlantic.com/magazine/archive/2019/06/trump-racism-comments/588067/

Grant, M. (1916). *The Passing of the Great Race or The Racial Basis of European History.* Charles Scribner's Sons.

H-1B Petitions by Gender and Country of Origin. (2018). *U.S. Citizenship and Immigration Services.* https://www.uscis.gov/sites/default/files/document/reports/h-1b-petitions-by-gender-country-of-birth-fy2018.pdf

Haltiwanger, J. (2018, April 30). Trump Doesn't Deny Calling African Countries 'Shitholes' While Meeting with Nigeria's President. *Business Insider.* https://www.businessinsider.com/trump-doesnt-deny-calling-african-countries-shitholes-2018-4

Harvey, J. (2023, August 17). Ex-Trump Aide Says Trump's use of Word 'Riggers' Is a Racist Dog Whistle. *HuffPost.* https://news.yahoo.com/ex-trump-aide-says-trumps-121011539.html

Helderman, R. S. (2022, October 16). Trump Attacks American Jews, Posted They Must 'Get Their Act Together' on Israel. *The Washington Post.* https://www.washingtonpost.com/politics/2022/10/16/trump-jews-israel/

Hesson, T. (2023, May 30). Trump Vows to End Birthright Citizenship for Children of Immigrants in US Illegally. *Reuters.* https://www.reuters.com/world/us/trump-vows-end-birthright-citizenship-children-immigrants-us-illegally-2023-05-30/

Hillyard, V., & Terkel, A. (2024, January 9). Trump Promotes 'Totally Baseless' Birther Conspiracy Theory Against Nikki Haley. *NBC News*. https://www.nbcnews.com/politics/donald-trump/trump-promotes-baseless-birther-conspiracy-theory-nikki-haley-rcna133166

Horwitz, S., & Sacchetti, M. (2018, May 7). Sessions Vows to Prosecute All Illegal Border Crosses and Separate Children from Their Parents. *The Washington Post*. https://www.washingtonpost.com/world/national-security/sessions-says-justice-dept-will-prosecute-every-person-who-crosses-border-unlawfully/2018/05/07/e1312b7e-5216-11e8-9c91-7dab596e8252_story.html

How it happened: Donald Trump's 'sh*thole countries' Remark. (2018, January 12). *CBS News*. https://www.cbsnews.com/news/how-it-happened-donald-trumps-shithole-countries-remark/

Iseman, M. St. W. (1912). *Race Suicide*. The Cosmopolitan Press.

Jackson, D. (2018, January 12). Trump appears to deny using vulgar term to describe immigrant countries after backlash. *USA Today*. https://www.usatoday.com/story/news/politics/2018/01/12/trump-denies-sort-cifer/1027493001/

Jeshion, R. (2013). Expressivism and the Offensiveness of Slurs. *Philosophical Perspectives, 27*, 231–259.

Johnson, J., & Hauslohner, A. (2017, May 20). 'I Think Islam Hates Us': A Timeline of Trump's Comments About Islam and Muslims. *The Washington Post*. https://www.washingtonpost.com/news/post-politics/wp/2017/05/20/i-think-islam-hates-us-a-timeline-of-trumps-comments-about-islam-and-muslims/

Kahn, J., Darnovsky, M., & Marks, J. (2020, October 5). Trump's 'Racehorse Theory' and Why It Matters. *Biopolitical Times*. https://www.geneticsandsociety.org/biopolitical-times/trumps-racehorse-theory-and-why-it-matters

Kanno-Youngs, Z. (2020, January 31). Trump Administration Adds Six Countries to Travel Ban. *The New York Times*. https://www.nytimes.com/2020/01/31/us/politics/trump-travel-ban.html

Karni, A., & Altman, L. K. (2019, February 14). At 243 Pounds, Trump Tips the Scale Into Obesity. *The New York Times*. https://www.nytimes.com/2019/02/14/us/politics/trump-obese.html

Kaufman, W. (2016, January 21). Woody Guthrie, 'Old Man Trump' and a Real Estate Empire's Racist Foundations. *The Conversation*. https://theconversation.com/woody-guthrie-old-man-trump-and-a-real-estate-empires-racist-foundations-53026

Kendall, B. (2016, June 3). Trump Says Judge's Mexican Heritage Presents 'Absolute Conflict.' *The Wall Street Journal*. https://www.wsj.com/articles/donald-trump-keeps-up-attacks-on-judge-gonzalo-curiel-1464911442

Kertscher, T. (2016, June 8). Donald Trump's Racial Comments about Hispanic Judge in Trump University Case. *Politifact*. https://www.politifact.com/art icle/2016/jun/08/donald-trumps-racial-comments-about-judge-trump-un/

Kettner, J. H. (1978). *The Development of American Citizenship 1608–1870*. The University of North Carolina Press.

Kitchener, C., Dawsey, J., & Knowles, H. (2024, January 5). Trump Wins Back Antiabortion Movement as Activists Plot 2025 Crackdowns. *The Washington Post*. https://www.washingtonpost.com/politics/2024/01/05/trump-abortion/

Kohlman, M. (2014, July 29). Nordicism. *Eugenics Archive*. http://eugenicsa rchive.ca/discover/tree/53d82b204c879d0000000001

Korecki, N., & Edelman, A. (2024, April 11). Trump's Conflicting Abortion Stances Are Coming Back to Haunt Him—And His Party. *NBC News*. https://www.nbcnews.com/politics/donald-trump/trumps-abortion-stances-republicans-2024-gop-rcna147222

Kranish, M. (2020, May 4). Trump Says He Shares His Famed Uncle's Science Genius. A Friend Says The Uncle 'Would Have Been Horrified.' *The Washington Post*. https://www.washingtonpost.com/politics/trump-says-he-sha res-his-famed-uncles-science-genius-a-friend-says-the-uncle-would-have-been-horrified/2020/05/03/76f58726-898e-11ea-9759-6d20ba0f2c0e_story.html

Ladd-Taylor, M. (2017). *Fixing the Poor: Eugenical Sterilization and Child Welfare in the Twentieth Century*. Johns Hopkins University Press.

Laughlin, H. H. (1922, November 21). Analysis of America's Modern Melting Pot. Remarks in Hearings Before the House Committee on Immigration and Naturalization. Sixty-Seventh Congress, Third session.

Laughlin, H. H. (1920, April 16–17). Biological Aspects of Immigration. Remarks in Hearings Before the House Committee on Immigration and Naturalization. Sixty-Sixth Congress, Second Session.

Layne, N., & Reid, T. (2023, October 17). Trump pledges to expel immigrants to support Hamas, ban Muslims from the U.S. Reuters. https://www.reu ters.com/world/us/trump-pledges-expel-immigrants-who-support-hamas-ban-muslims-us-2023-10-16/

LeBeuf, L. G. (1904). The Attitude of the Medical Profession Towards Race Suicide and Criminal Abortion. *The New Orleans Medical and Surgical Journal, 57*, 3–18.

Lebowitz, M., & Traylor, J. (2024, March 4). Trump Compares Migrants to Hannibal Lecter in 'The Silence of the Lambs.' *NBC*. https://www.nbc news.com/politics/donald-trump/trump-compares-migrants-hannibal-lecter-silence-lambs-rcna141792

Lebowitz, M. (2024, March 18). Trump Says Jews Who Vote for Democrats 'Hate' Israel and 'Their Religion.' *NBC News*. https://www.nbcnews.com/politics/donald-trump/trump-says-jews-vote-democrats-hate-israel-religion-rcna143988

Leingang, R. (2024, April 6). Trump's Bizarre, Vindictive Incoherence Has to Be Heard in Full to be Believed. *The Guardian*. https://www.theguardian.com/us-news/2024/apr/06/donald-trump-speech-analysis

Leon, S. M. (2013). *An Image of God: The Catholic Struggle with Eugenics*. The University of Chicago Press.

Leung, C. (2014, April 29). Popular Culture. *Eugenics Archive*. https://eugenicsarchive.ca/discover/connections/535eed7a7095aa000000024a

LeVine, M. (2023, November 12). Trump Calls Political Enemies 'Vermin.' Echoing Dictators Hitler, Mussolini. *The Washington Post*. https://www.washingtonpost.com/politics/2023/11/12/trump-rally-vermin-political-opponents/

Lindsay, M. (1998). Reproducing a Fit Citizenry: Dependency, Eugenics, and the Law of Marriage in the United States, 1860–1920. *Law & Social Inquiry*, *23*(3), 541–585.

Lintelman, J. K. (2019). Swedish Immigration to Minnesota. *MNopedia*. https://www.mnopedia.org/swedish-immigration-minnesota

Liptak, A. (2021, August 24). Supreme Court Allows Revival of Trump-Era 'Remain in Mexico' Asylum Policy. *The New York Times*. https://www.nytimes.com/2021/08/24/us/politics/supreme-court-immigration-asylum-mexico.html

List of Nicknames Used by Donald Trump. (2024, April 11). In *Wikipedia*. https://en.wikipedia.org/wiki/List_of_nicknames_used_by_Donald_Trump

Lopez, G. (2020, August 13). Donald Trump's Long History of Racism, from the 1970s to 2020. *Vox*. https://www.vox.com/2016/7/25/12270880/donald-trump-racist-racism-history

Lutz, E. (2023, November 27). Donald Trump's Abortion About-Face Is Cynical as Ever. *Vanity Fair*. https://www.vanityfair.com/news/2023/11/donald-trump-abortion-strategy

Mackey, R. (2017, January 9). Beneath Trump's Mockery of a Reporter, a Cascade of Lies Leading Back to 9/11. *The Intercept*. https://theintercept.com/2017/01/09/trumps-lie-watching-celebrations-911-lurks-beneath-mockery-reporter/

Mahler, J., & Eder, S. (2016, August 27). 'No Vacancies' for Blacks: How Donald Trump Got His Start, and Was First Accused of Bias. *The New York Times*. https://www.nytimes.com/2016/08/28/us/politics/donald-trump-housing-race.html

Marcin, T. (2017, December 23). Trump Said Haitians Have AIDS, Nigerians Live in Huts in Oval Office Meeting, New York Times Reports. *Newsweek*. https://www.newsweek.com/trump-haitians-aids-nigerians-live-huts-oval-office-new-york-times-report-758000

Martinez, A. A. (2017, January 1). Fred Trump and the KKK. *New Standard Press*. http://www.newstandardpress.com/fred-trump-and-the-kkk/

McCarthy, T. (2018, May 2). Trump Dictated Note Saying He Was 'Astonishingly' Healthy, Doctor Says. *The Guardian.* https://www.theguardian.com/us-news/2018/may/01/trump-dictated-doctors-note-harold-bornstein

McPhillips, D. (2023, November 21). Births Have Increased in States with Abortion Bans, Research Finds. *CNN.* https://www.cnn.com/2023/11/21/health/abortion-bans-increase-births/index.html

Mehta, S. (2020, October 5). Trump's Touting of 'Racehorse Theory' Tied to Eugenics and Nazis Alarms Jewish Leaders. *Los Angeles Times.* https://www.latimes.com/politics/story/2020-10-05/trump-debate-white-supremacy-racehorse-theory

Morales, C., Waller, A., & Fazio, M. (2020, October 4). A Timeline of Trump's Symptoms and Treatments. *The New York Times.* https://www.nytimes.com/2020/10/04/us/trump-covid-symptoms-timeline.html

Mortimer, C. (2016, September 30). Donald Trump Believes He Has Superior Genes, Biographer Claims. *Independent.* https://www.independent.co.uk/news/world/americas/donald-trump-president-superior-genes-pbs-documentary-eugenics-a7338821.html

Muller, R.-D., & Ueberschar, G. R. (2002). *Hitler's War in the East, 1941–1945: A Critical Assessment.* Berghahn Books.

Nickel, D. (2021, April 9). The Scandinavian American Story. *Life in Norway.* https://www.lifeinnorway.net/scandinavian-american/

Norton, T. (2022, September 23). Fact Check: Did Trump's Phone Correct 'Racist Slur' About Letitia James? *Newsweek.* https://www.newsweek.com/fact-check-did-trumps-phone-correct-racist-slur-about-letitia-james-1745736

Norwegian Population by State. (2024). *World Population Review.* https://worldpopulationreview.com/state-rankings/norwegian-population-by-state)

O'Donnell, C. (2020, October 9). Timeline: History of Trump's COVID-19 Illness. *Reuters.* https://www.reuters.com/article/us-health-coronavirus-trump-timeline/timeline-history-of-trumps-covid-19-illness-idUSKBN26U299

Ordover, N. (2003). *American Eugenics: Race, Queer Anatomy, and the Science of Nationalism.* University of Minnesota Press.

Papenfuss, M. (2021, September 5). Trump Gripes About Losing Ungrateful Catholic, Jewish Voters on Call with Religious Advisers. *Yahoo!News.* https://news.yahoo.com/trump-gripes-losing-ungrateful-catholic-065654358.html

Pernick, M. S. (1997). Eugenics and Public Health in American History. *American Journal of Public Health, 87*(11), 1767–1772.

Putney, C. (2001). *Muscular Christianity: Manhood and Sports in Protestant America, 1880–1920.* Harvard University Press.

Quinn, P. A. (1995, February 18). Immigration's Dark History. *America: The Jesuit Review.* https://www.americamagazine.org/issue/100/immigrations-dark-history

Rappeport, A. (2016, June 3). That Judge Attacked by Donald Trump? He's Faced a Lot Worse. *The New York Times.* https://www.nytimes.com/2016/06/04/us/politics/donald-trump-university-judge-gonzalo-curiel.html

Rieger, J. M. (2019, August 5). When a Rallygoer Suggested Shooting Immigrants in May, Trump Made a Joke. *The Washington Post.* https://www.washingtonpost.com/politics/2019/08/05/when-rally-goer-suggested-shooting-immigrants-may-trump-made-joke/

Rosenberg, Y. (2023, September 19). Trump's Menacing Rosh Hashanah Message to American Jews. *The Atlantic.* https://www.theatlantic.com/ideas/archive/2023/09/trumps-menacing-rosh-hashanah-message-to-american-jews/675367/

Saleeby, C. (1909). *Parenthood and Race Culture.* Cassell and Co.

Scott, E. (2015, July 2). Trump Defends Inflammatory Comments, asks 'Who Is Doing the Raping?' *CNN.* https://www.cnn.com/2015/07/01/politics/donald-trump-immigrants-raping-comments/index.html

Shear, M. D., & Davis, J. H. (2017, December 23). Stoking Fears, Trump Defied Bureaucracy to Advance Immigration Agenda. *The New York Times.* https://www.nytimes.com/2017/12/23/us/politics/trump-immigration.html

Sixth Annual Message. (1906, December 3). *The American Presidency Project.* https://www.presidency.ucsb.edu/documents/sixth-annual-message-4

Smith, A. (2019, August 21). Trump Doubles Down on Calling Jewish Democrats 'Disloyal' to Israel. *NBC News.* https://www.nbcnews.com/politics/donald-trump/trump-doubles-down-calling-jewish-democrats-disloyal-israel-n1044861

Smith, D. (2018, January 16). White House Doctor Says Trump Will Remain 'Fit for Duty' for Years. *The Guardian.* https://www.theguardian.com/us-news/2018/jan/16/white-house-doctor-says-trump-is-in-excellent-overall-health

Smith, D. (2020, December 07). Earnest Sevier Cox (1880–1966). In *Encyclopedia Virginia.* https://encyclopediavirginia.org/entries/cox-earnest-sevier-1880-1966

Smith, G. A. (2024, March 15). 5 Facts about Religion and Americans' Views of Donald Trump. *Pew Research Center.* https://www.pewresearch.org/short-reads/2024/03/15/5-facts-about-religion-and-americans-views-of-donald-trump/

Smith-Schoenwalder, C. (2024, April 8). Quotes: Comparing Trump's Stance on Abortion Over Time. *US News & World Report.* https://www.usnews.com/news/national-news/articles/2024-01-11/quotes-comparing-trumps-stance-on-abortion-over-time

Stoddard, L. (1920). *The Rising Tide of Color Against White World-Supremacy.* Charles Scribner's Sons.

Stoddard, L. (1922). *The Revolt Against Civilization: The Menace of the Under Man.* Charles Scribner's Sons.

Stoddard, L. (1924). *Racial Realities in Europe*. Charles Scribner's Sons.
Stoddard, L. (1940). *Into the Darkness: Nazi Germany Today*. Duell, Sloan & Pearce, Incorporated
The H-1B Visa Program. (2021, May 26). *American Immigration Council*. https://www.americanimmigrationcouncil.org/research/h1b-visa-program-fact-sheet
Trump Said the People of Minnesota Have 'Good Genes.' (2020, September 21). *Yahoo!News*. https://www.yahoo.com/now/trump-said-people-minnesota-good-170345603.html
Turx, J. (2021, June 16). Exclusive: Donald J. Trump's Winter White House // Catching Up With the 45th President Ahead of His Departure from Mar-a-Lago. *Ami Magazine*. https://www.amimagazine.org/2021/06/16/donald-j-trumps-winter-white-house/
Vazquez, M. (2019, August 16). Trump Called Supporter After Mocking Him During a Rally Over a 'Serious Weight Problem.' *CNN Politics*. https://www.cnn.com/2019/08/16/politics/donald-trump-supporter-weight-new-hampshire-rally/index.html
Wade, P. (2024, March 17). Trump Escalates His Dehumanization of Migrants: Some Are 'Not People... These Are Animals.' *Rolling Stone*. https://www.yahoo.com/news/trump-escalates-dehumanization-migrants-not-144030563.html
Watson, K., & Hudak, Z. (2023, July 7). Trump Says He'd Bring Back 'Travel Ban' That's Even Bigger Than Before. *CBS News*. https://www.cbsnews.com/news/trump-bring-back-travel-ban-muslim-countries/
Weikart, R. (2004). *From Darwin to Hitler: Evolutionary Ethics, Eugenics, and Racism in Germany*. Palgrave Macmillan.
Weiland, N., Haberman, M., Mazzetti, M., & Karni, A. (2021, February 11). Trump Was Sicker Than Acknowledged with Covid-19. *The New York Times*. https://www.nytimes.com/2021/02/11/us/politics/trump-coronavirus.html
Zezima, K., & DelReal, J. A. (2016, September 28). Donald Trump's Weight Problem: He Can't Stop Talking About 'Fat' People. *The Washington Post*. https://www.washingtonpost.com/politics/donald-trumps-weight-problem-he-cant-stop-talking-about-fat-people/2016/09/28/891ddd3a-858d-11e6-a3ef-f35afb41797f_story.html
Zurski, K. (2021, May 19). The Nimrod Effect: How a Cartoon Bunny Changed the Meaning of a Word Forever. *UnRemembered*. https://unrememberedhistory.com/2017/01/09/the-nimrod-effect-how-a-cartoon-bunny-changed-the-meaning-of-a-word-forever/

CHAPTER 5

Conclusion

Abstract The concluding chapter summarizes aspects of the previous chapters and attempts to frame them in context. The book focuses on the power of eugenics. It explores how the language and ideas of famous eugenicists still impact us today. Their ideas, thoughts, and beliefs shaped and continue to shape our world. They influence our ideas about immigration, acceptance, and belonging within America. Donald Trump's rhetoric suggests he embraces many positions stridently advocated by early twentieth-century American eugenicists.

Keywords Donald Trump · Presidential rhetoric · Immigration · Citizen versus subject · Eugenics

Power. Who has it, who controls it, and how is it used? Societies revolve around power. As children in America, one of the first board games we learned to play was Monopoly. After losing a few times, we discovered one of the best paths to winning involves stacking houses and hotels on your most valuable properties. The other players dread and fear you if you control enough of the board because you can bankrupt everyone else or let their bad roll slide. That's power. Power controls the game. The ones in power set the rules and help guide others toward desirable outcomes.

Eugenics gave people a way to posture superiority while draping a supposed scientific veneer over it, creating an aura of truthiness. They crafted a narrative that White Northern Europeans were the paramount exemplars of genetic and social life for the entirety of the Earth. Eugenics then provided a path to cultivate that answer by backward engineering history and cherry-picking science to make that conclusion seem logical. It was a fallacy. It was, in its way, historical self-insert fanfiction before we had terms for it.

Eugenics allows for bigotry to masquerade as objective science. The irony with eugenics is much of it started in a noble place, wanting to improve the lives of people in poverty. However, to paraphrase Bugs Bunny, it took a wrong turn at Albuquerque and quickly shifted into a way to justify discrimination based on social class, ethnicity, disability, and race. The United States has been permanently altered by eugenics. Many policies, ranging from marriage, sterilization, immigration, and even political participation, have been impacted by these attitudes. Eugenics opened up ways to demonize people who did not accept their principles as flawed moral failures existing as less worthy within society. Their perspectives mainstreamed their biases into policy and normalized them as acceptable platforms.

This book attempts to explain eugenics' development, longevity, and persistence within American society. The origins of eugenics began in the second half of the nineteenth century. Urbanism throughout the United Kingdom and the United States had many people living near each other in concentrated areas. Some of the very earliest works in eugenics sought to try to improve the lives of people with issues like alcoholism. The ability to mitigate causes and outcomes associated with alcoholism would result in more efficient, productive, and healthy populations.

Unfortunately, scientific understanding was extremely limited in these periods. Concepts like DNA were not even dreamed of at this point, leading people to move toward ideas that carefully selected breeding results in better populations. Unsurprisingly, the best populations for ideal human reproduction were the same ones who developed these ideas. The first chapter of this book explains how ideas contained within eugenics are simultaneously old and new. Ideas like conscientious reproduction are present within Plato, but other far more modern ideas like Calvinism helped invoke and inculcate these ideas in early America. Eugenics mainstreamed within America by piggybacking on agricultural fairs. Farmers understood the concepts of responsible animal husbandry. Careful selection of their crop and stocks often displayed preferred genomic characteristics. It was a relatively easy leap toward applying the same ideas to humans when deftly framed in specific ways. Fitter Family and Better Baby contests played toward reinforcing vanity while espousing eugenic ideals to propagate the best human stock.

The primary theme throughout the book involves the impact of the Immigration Act of 1924 on the United States. This legislation became law at the height of eugenics. Many of the chapters address the importance of this act on our country. The first chapter introduces it and simultaneously highlights it in context with other things in America. The Second International Congress on Eugenics was held in New York City in 1921, and many of its exhibitions moved to the U.S. Capitol for display. Persons heavily involved in the eugenics movement, such as Harry Laughlin, testified in front of Congress about immigration policy. The next chapter, primarily about mammy statues, may initially feel disjointed, but the connection is pertinent and essential. The United Daughters of the Confederacy wanted congressional assistance and authorization to place a mammy statue in Washington, D.C. This legislation was in roughly the same time frame as immigration restriction testimony along with eugenic displays in the Capitol. Mammy statues are not simply monuments. They are physical representations of sanctioned behavior and mannerisms.

Chapter two presents the origin and growth of the movement toward creating faithful slave memorials, especially mammies within the United States. Political figures were the first ones to advocate for these statues. Some of the loudest advocates for these monuments were simultaneously attempting to withhold political rights and participation from Black Americans. The statues are not just images but idealizations of accepted behaviors for persons of color within American society. They offered a fictionalized narrative that was retconned for people to believe it as the truth over reality. Immigration restrictions were on the minds of Congress, and these memorials were also up for consideration. Immigration was not acted on until the next session, but it did influence hearings, attitudes, and agenda setting in the same period as mammy statuary issues.

The third chapter expands on these concepts of immigration by tracing historical immigration paths in this country. Many people who embrace eugenics and American nativism arrived via their ancestors' forced transportation during the colonial period as felons from the United Kingdom.

Over time, they reinvented their ancestry as one of an imperious nature. They embraced the folk stories of the American founding, claimed them as their own, and held them as the sterling benchmark for all new immigrants to measure themselves against for worthiness.

Restrictive immigration policies began during the second half of the nineteenth century. Many of the most adherent advocates pushed for the elimination of all non-White social groups. In particular, they embraced Nordicism as the epitome and pushed to refashion American society in that ethnic image. Racial and ethnic fears and concerns were entangled in the passage of the 1924 legislation that heavily restricted immigration and placed quotas on most of the world's population.

The fourth chapter explores how Donald Trump acts in ways that suggest he has embraced and also rebranded historical eugenics into mainstream platforms and policy. Many things he has stated as a presidential candidate and president are strikingly similar to early twentieth-century eugenicists and their beliefs. The chapter analyzes many of his statements and places them in context with similar ideals and phrases espoused by authors and persons associated with the United States eugenics movement. The chapter also explores his tactic of using slurs to weaponize rhetoric. Donald Trump has taken the presidential tool of going public (Kernell, 1987) and shifted it from a way to pressure institutions into a technique to target individuals. He has personalized going public by weaponizing it against people he wants to bend to his will. Weaponized going public has turned the bully pulpit into a pulpit for bullies. Donald Trump uses very different sorts of slurs toward women of color compared to White men and women. He adopts terms that almost always take on a negative racial tinge. They normalize flattening women of color into a two-dimensional caricature in similar ways mammy statues sought to do the same thing. Donald Trump presents himself as healthy and vital and plays right into eugenic tropes of health and fitness. His views on religiosity also conform to eugenic beliefs about subjects, citizenry, and behavior.

Detractors often dismiss Donald Trump's statements and beliefs as hyperbolic racist bluster. When people do that, they negate his words' seriousness and historical grounding. His own words suggest his attitudes are consistent with the eugenic ancestry of the United States. Our country spent much of the latter half of the nineteenth century through the mid-twentieth century negating political rights, voices, participation, and the ability for many persons of color to immigrate. Adherents of eugenics crafted a pseudoscientific narrative that, on the surface, looked rational but was born from biases and bigotry. Their choices, decisions, and policies determined who was allowed and never allowed to immigrate. Acceptance in all its forms for persons of color hinged upon creating a non-threatening image that did not intimidate those in power. Donald Trump rarely uses humor in his rhetoric (Zoglin, 2020). His words and statements must always be taken at face value because he means them that way. Donald Trump's speech content often appears to contain thought balloons to see if they garner traction. His actions suggest negative feedback results in their removal, looking as if he wants to tabula rasa, or in golfing terms, claim a mulligan to avoid accountability.

Donald Trump acts as if he sees the world through a distinct eugenic lens. Ethnicity, race, and nationality bequeath more value than personal character. A person's ancestry provides more insight into their value than their accomplishments. Their value to society resides within their blood rather than experience, education, or ethical behavior. Adherents to eugenics justify their attitudes by demonizing others with cherry-picked examples that play to fear-mongering to compel abeyance. Whataboutisms are rife in their rhetorical toolkit to derail any factual discussions. It is easier to engage in logical fallacies and shift away from being forced to provide any evidence for their assertions. Donald Trump's words suggest he plays to his audience's vanity by offering them the ability to cast themselves as patriotic victims without personal accountability for their circumstances. Everything negative in their world can be attributed to amorphous others rather than their individual choices and decisions.

Donald Trump's repetitive use of eugenic-based language (see Chapter 4) allows for the exploitation of classic eugenic tropes to voice anxieties for those who have seen their racial and ethnic dominance slide in the second half of the twentieth and first quarter of the twenty-first centuries. Eugenics, however, has never offered meaningful, inclusive solutions. It often appeals to the fantasies of the 'good ol' days.' Sections of this book, particularly within Chapters 2 and 3, have attempted to highlight how these worlds never truly existed. They are mythos passed across dinner tables to make familial origin stories feel more grandiose and significant.

Eugenics offered the world idealized societies free from want, shortcomings, and disease. It plays to people's vanity. The reality could never deliver on the promises. Eugenic solutions involve creating as many people of their preferred group as possible by marginalizing everyone else. These goals can be achieved through blanket immigration restrictions, societal isolation, and sterilization or elimination of everyone who is not an exemplar from their breeding stock.

Voting and political participation within the world of eugenics exist as highly regulated activities. Chapter 2 explained how the 1901 Alabama Constitutional Convention discussed in idealized terms the creation of a statue of a mammy while also explicitly framing itself as a way to "establish white supremacy in this State" ("Journal," 1901, p. 9) and disenfranchise black voters. As noted in Chapter 4, citizens and subjects often have different rights within a society. Citizens participate in decision-making, whereas subjects are governed and given limited rights. Advocates of the removal of birthright citizenship seek to turn these persons into subjects to curtail constitutional rights. The citizen versus subject argument strikes at the very heart of what it means to be an American. Subjects do not have the same ability to expect full protection of rights. When politicians or others assert the 14th Amendment does not convey birthright citizenship, they are denoting segments of the population into subject status. Citizenship becomes a commodity managed by an elite class. Privileged elites receive it automatically, but others are not conferred the same rights unless those in power see fit to bestow that status upon them.

When the horrors of the World War II Holocaust became known, eugenics began to see a decline in popularity. We often associate the concentration camps of the Holocaust with the systematic elimination of Jewish people. However, while they were a large targeted population, they were not the only group affected by systemic eugenic incarceration and elimination by the Third Reich. Homosexuals, Roma, persons with disabilities, Polish, Slavs, people of African descent, as well as others, were also considered inferior to the Third Reich and were detained and often sent to concentration camps.

Our world worked hard to improve social science, attitudes, and understanding after this war. Governmental policies based on pseudoscience eventually received careful critical attention and examination for their inherent flaws. The Hart-Celler Act of 1965 changed America's 1924 immigration laws and started to move us past its built-in biases.

On August 28, 1963, Martin Luther King, Jr. gave his famous 'I Have a Dream' speech at the Lincoln Memorial in Washington, DC. Within this speech, he says, "I have a dream that my four little children will one day live in a nation where they will not be judged by the color of their skin but by the content of their character" ("Read," 2023). American society holds this speech up as one of the most important and formative of the twentieth century. King discusses the need for equality within American life. This book attempts to build a story to help explain the persistence and lingering aspects of eugenics within the United States. His speech often is interpreted as a call for equality and freedom, asking people to judge others on their merits rather than their superficial differences. While true, there may also exist a deeper meaning in King's words. Asking society to judge others by the content of their character rather than their skin tone directly challenges the heart of eugenic beliefs. King perhaps understood eugenics was not eliminated in the aftermath of World War II but transitioned into an unspoken reality. Attitudes and beliefs lingered, but it was unacceptable to say them out loud. Within this quote, King seems to call for a new America, not shackled by eugenic ideals, but one where individual merit and accomplishment reign paramount.

REFERENCES

Journal of the Alabama Constitutional Convention of 1901. (1901). *Alabama Department of Archives & History.* https://digital.archives.alabama.gov/digital/collection/constitutions/id/116/

Kernell, S. (1987). *Going Public: New Strategies of Presidential Leadership.* CQ Press.

Read Martin Luther King Jr.'s 'I Have a Dream' speech in its entirety. (2023, January 16). *NPR.* https://www.npr.org/2010/01/18/122701268/i-have-a-dream-speech-in-its-entirety

Zoglin, R. (2020, July 5). Why Do None of Trump's 'Jokes' Feel Like Jokes? *The Washington Post.* https://www.washingtonpost.com/opinions/why-do-none-of-trumps-jokes-feel-like-jokes/2020/07/03/bdcc053a-bca1-11ea-bdaf-a129f921026f_story.html

Index

A
abortion, 10
Act of Regulate Immigration, 64
Adams, John, 58
Alabama Constitutional Convention, 31, 118
alcoholism, 4
Alien and Sedition Acts, 61
American Community Survey, 64
American Museum of National History, 47
Arlington Confederate Monument Association, 38
Arnold, Matthew, 79
Arnold, Thomas, 79
Asiatic Barred Zone, 66

B
Bach family, 79
back-to-nature movement, 16
Bacon, Selden, 5
Balibar, E., 91
Battle Creek Sanitarium, 11
Baum, Arthur J., 34

Better Baby Contest, 13, 14
Biddle, Anthony Drexel, 9
Biden, Joe, 79, 94, 100
Black Mammy Memorial Institute, 33, 48
Blake, Eloise, 36, 37
Boy Scouts, 16
Brandegee, Frank B., 42
Brown, Mary, 3
Bryan, Jackson Lee, 44
Buck v. Bell, 20
Bugs Bunny, 114
Bureau of the Census, 18
Burger King, 76
Butler, J.D., 60

C
Cable Act, 65
Calvin, Ira, xi, 93, 94
Calvinism, ix, 6–8, 114
Cambridge University, 79
Campbell, M., 60
Campfire Girls, 16
Carlisle, 40

© The Editor(s) (if applicable) and The Author(s), under exclusive license to Springer Nature Switzerland AG 2024
S. B. O'Brien, *Eugenics in American Political Life*,
https://doi.org/10.1007/978-3-031-63553-3

Cheney, Liz, 96
Chinese Exclusion Act, 64
Chow, Elaine, 96
Clay, Pauline, 37
Clinton, Hillary, 96
Committee on the Library
 House, 42
 Joint, 42
 Senate, 42
Confederate Memorial at Arlington National Cemetery, 37–40
Coolidge, Calvin, 69
Cox, Earnest, 80
Crane, R. Newton, 12
Curiel, Gonzalo, 89
Curtis, George William, 18

D
Darwin, Charles, 3, 4, 79
Darwin, Erasmus, 79
Davenport, Charles, 3
Davidson, Frank E., 46
Davis, Jefferson, 38
DeJarnette, Joseph, 21
Dobbs v. Jackson Women's Health Organization, 86, 87
Donald Trump and the Kayfabe Presidency, viii
Dorr, Gregory, 6
Durban, Dick, 78

E
Elderton, Ethel M., 4
Eliot, Charles William, 79
Emergency Immigration Act of 1921, 68
Emergency Quota Act of 1921, 69
Eugenics Laboratory, 4
Eugenics Records Office, 18, 66
Eugenics Society of Northern California, 5

Evans, Hiram Wesley, 68
Evening Star, 41
Expatriation Act, 1907, 65

F
fairs, 13–15
 awards, 14
 circus, 15
 sideshow, 15
 sideshows, 14
 wrestling acts, 15
Felon, Transported, 56–60
Fetal Alcohol Spectrum Disorders, 5
Fetal Alcohol Syndrome. *See* Fetal Alcohol Spectrum Disorders
Fitter Family Contest, 13
Fourteenth Amendment, 82, 83
French Revolution, 61

G
Galton, Francis, xi, 3, 4, 79
Galton Laboratory, 4
Gamboa, S., 92
Gaustad, Edwin, 7
Geary Act, 65
going public, 116
Gone with the Wind, 28
Good Darky. *See* Uncle Jack
Gould, Norman, 42
Grant, Madison, xi, 66, 68, 77, 78, 82, 83, 90
Griffith, Alyssa Farah, 94
Griswold v. Connecticut, 87
Groce, T.J., 34
Guthrie, Woody, 77
Guyer, Michael, 20

H
H-1B visas, 92, 93
Haley, Nikki, 83, 95, 96
Hampden-Sidney, 40

Harriman, Mary Williamson Averell, 18
Harris, Thomas, 90
Hart-Celler Act of 1965, 118
Harvard University, 40
Heflin, James Thomas, 31–33, 48
Herbert, Hilary A., 38
Hill, Joseph A., 68
Hitler, Adolf, xi, 2, 81, 91, 94
Holocaust, 118
Hood's Brigade, 30
Horsley, J.S., 12
Hutchinson, William, 7

I
Immigration Act, 1891, 65
Immigration Act, 1907, 65
Immigration Act, 1917, 66, 96
Immigration Act of 1924, x, 46, 68, 69, 71, 79, 82, 90, 96, 115
Johnson-Reed Act, 66
Immigration and Nationality Act of 1952, 96
Irish Rebellion of 1798, 61
Iseman, Myre St. Wald, 10

J
Jackson, Andrew, 62
Jackson, Stonewall, 45
James, Letitia, 95, 96
Jefferson, Thomas, 6, 8
Jemima, Aunt, 28
Jeshion, R., 95
Johnson, Albert, 66
Johnson, Alexander, 12
Johnson-Reed Act. *See* Immigration Act of 1924
Immigration Act of 1924, 46
Jones, Richard Channing, 32

K
Kellogg, John Harvey, 9, 11
Kennedy, John F., 101
Kercher, B., 58
King, Jr., Martin Luther, 118, 119
Kingsley, Charles, 79
Klu Klux Klan, 68, 77
Knox, John B., 32

L
Lampton, Edward Wilkinson, 36
Laughlin, Harry, xi, 8, 19, 20, 46, 47, 66, 68, 70, 77, 80, 91, 115
Laughlin laws, 20
Lawrence v. Texas, 87
Lemon, Don, 88
Lens, Fritz, 70
Lidbetter, E.J., 18
Lieber, Francis, 60
Lombroso, Cesare, 88
Louisiana State University in Baton Rouge
Rural Life Museum, 44
Louisiana Tourist Bureau, 44

M
Mammy, 28, 30–33, 35–37, 39–42, 48
Mammy statue, ix, x, 28, 30, 33–36, 40, 41, 43, 46–48, 80, 115
Marse Chan. *See* Page, Thomas Nelson
Masaryk, Thomas Garrigue, 43
Mayflower, 12
McDaniel, Hattie, 28
McDonald's, 76
McElya, Micki, 33, 40
Medico-Psychological Association of Great Britain and Ireland, 4
Mein Kampf. *See* Hitler, Adolf
Mervin, Henry C., 9

Mill, James, 79
Mill, John Stuart, 79
Moll Flanders, 12, 60
Monopoly, 113
Morgan, K., 59
Morris, Richard, 59
Murkowski, Lisa, 96
Muscular Christianity, 9, 98

N
National Manassas Battlefield, 45
Nazi, 1, 2, 21, 81, 101
Neustadt, Richard, viii
New Deal Coalition, 100
Newgate, 60
Newman, Omarosa Manigault, 96
New Market Battlefield State Historical Park, 40
Ngai, M.M., 68
1924 Immigration Acts, 19. *See also* Johnson-Reed Immigration Act
Nordicism, 19, 77, 78, 92, 116
Notes on the State of Virginia, 6

O
Obama, Barack, 83
Obergefell v. Hodges, 87
Ocasio-Cortez, Alexandria, 96
Old Black Mammy Monument Association, 34
Ordover, N., 91
Orebaugh, David A., 12

P
Page, Thomas Nelson, 38
Park, Frank, 42
Pauly, Philip J., 20
Pearson, Karl, 4
Pelosi, Nancy, 97
Plato, 3, 4, 114

Proctor, R.N., 70
Professional wrestling, ix
  smart marks, ix
Progressive Era, vii

R
Race Betterment Foundation, 11
racehorse theory, 77, 80
race suicide, x, 9, 10, 70, 84, 92
Reichstag, 20
Rentoul, Robert Reid, 10, 21
Rice, DeLong, 29
Roosevelt, Theodore, 9, 10, 84–87
  race suicide, 84
Rosen, Jacky, 97
Ross, Edward, 9

S
Saleeby, Caleb, 79
Santa Claus, 48
Schweizer, Ada E., 13
Scott, James C., 44
Second International Congress, 18
Second International Congress on Eugenics, 47, 115
Sedgwick, William T., 17
servants, indentured, 60
Sheridan, Philip, 29, 30
Silence of the Lambs, 90
Sixty-Eighth Congress, 42
Sixty-Seventh Congress, 42, 43
Smith, Al, 101
Southern Poverty Law Center, 35
Stedman, Charles, 41–43
Stern, Alexandra Minna, 21
Stillé, C.J., 60
Stoddard, Lothrop, xi, 66–68, 78, 80–82, 88, 93
Stowe, Harriet Beecher, 44

T

Taylor, Alfred, 28, 29
Taylor, Robert Love, 28–31
Terman, Lewis Madison, 21, 22
Terrell, Mary Church, 41
Third Reich, xi, 1, 2, 70, 77, 81, 82, 118
  Hereditary Health Court, 81
Thomas, Clarence, 87
Trump, Donald, vii–xi, 2, 21, 71, 76–80, 82–96, 98–101, 116, 117
  anchor babies, 83
  birthright citizenship, 82
  immigration policy, 84
  visa restrictions, 85
Trump, Fred, 76, 77
Trump, John, 79
Trump University, 89

U

Uncle Jack, 43
Uncle Tom's Cabin, 44
Undesirable Aliens Act, 69
United Daughters of the Confederacy, 29, 37, 40, 41, 43, 48, 115
University College London, 4
University of Berlin, 88

V

van Luschan, Felix, 88

Virginia Act to Preserve Racial Integrity, 80
Virginia Sterilization Act of 1924, 20

W

Wald, Kenneth D., viii
Wallerstein, I., 91
Ward, Robert DeCourcy, 17, 18
Warner Bros, 96
War of the Roses, 29
Warren, Elizabeth, 96
Washington, George, 60
Waters, Maxine, 96
Watts, Mary T., 13
Weikart, R., 88
Whataboutism, 117
Whitmer, Gretchen, 97
Williams, John Sharp, 40, 42, 43, 48
Willis, Fani, 96
Wilson, Woodrow, 38
Woodcraft Indians, 16
Woodworth, Robert, 11
World War II, 1, 118
Wright, R.O., 65

Y

Young Men's Christian Organization, 9

SPRINGER NATURE

GPSR Compliance

The European Union's (EU) General Product Safety Regulation (GPSR) is a set of rules that requires consumer products to be safe and our obligations to ensure this.

If you have any concerns about our products, you can contact us on ProductSafety@springernature.com

In case Publisher is established outside the EU, the EU authorized representative is:

Springer Nature Customer Service Center GmbH
Europaplatz 3
69115 Heidelberg, Germany

The manufacturer's authorised representative in the EU is Springer Nature Customer Service Centre GmbH, Europaplatz 3, 69115 Heidelberg, Germany. If you have any concerns regarding our products, please contact ProductSafety@springernature.com

Printed and bound by CPI Group (UK) Ltd, Croydon, CR0 4YY
23/03/2026
02076355-0006